Where is the best place to plant willow?
Why is it that old churchyards always seem to have a gnarled old yew?
When did some of our native woodlands become so thin?
   To these and other questions about trees and the plant animal and human life that depends on them, this book gives some informed answers.
   Warriors and Guardians gives an invaluable account of the native trees of Scotland. In an age when our precious natural inheritance is under continual threat, the country's own species of trees should be ever more treasured.
   This book will be of interest to all who cherish trees and the plants and wildlife that depend on them — gardeners, visitors, naturalists, walkers, foresters, landowners and conservationists.
   And Hugh Fife has written about the human significance of our native trees. The language and lore that surround our warriors and guardians is a moving testament to our capacity to make sense of our world.

Hugh Fife is widely experienced in woodland matters as a forester, landscape gardener and as a conservationist. He lives and works in Argyll.

Warriors and Guardians

Warriors and Guardians

native Highland trees

Hugh Fife

First published 1994
Argyll Publishing
Glendaruel
Argyll PA22 3AE

British Library Cataloguing-in-Publication Data.
**A catalogue record for this book is available from the British
Library.**

ISBN 1 874640 65 3

Cover photographs Norman Russell
Illustrations Irene MacKenzie
Design and layout Omnis Computer Graphics, Ardfern, Argyll
Reprographics Cordfall, Civic Street, Glasgow
Printed and bound in Great Britain Martins the Printers,
Berwick-upon-Tweed

Acknowledgements

For their help in different ways in gathering material for this book, I would like to thank the following — Reforesting Scotland at The Old Mill House, Braes, Ullapool; Scottish Natural Heritage staff at Lochgilphead; Marion Campbell of Kilberry, Argyll; Hugh Graham (born 1906) at Ballanoch, Argyll; Forest Enterprise staff at Lochgilphead and Rennie McOwan.

Hugh Fife

Contents

Foreword

While it is intended that this study of trees is easily read unhampered by botanical jargon some explanation of such terms used may be needed.

The texture and appearance of bark varies a great deal. Bark that is rough and cracked is called 'fissured'.

Some trees multiply by sending new shoots up from the roots. These new, young trees are called 'suckers'.

Many of our native trees continue to grow after felling, even when cut at ground level. The word for this growth — sometimes many narrow stems, sometimes just two or three wide limbs — is 'coppice'. 'Coppice' has a number of related meanings. As a noun it can mean the new growth or it can mean an area of trees producing growth after cutting. As a verb it can mean the act of cutting to produce coppice — 'coppicing' — and even the act of cutting the coppice growth.

The term 'self-sterile' describes a tree that, though producing flowers of both sexes on one individual, cannot produce fertile seeds: the pollen of the male flower must find a female flower on another individual.

I have introduced the terms 'forest tree' and 'non-forest tree' to simplify description of habitats. A non-forest tree may well grow in a forest, for instance the holly, but not as a forest, such as the oak.

Gaelic terms, like the individual tree names, are generally to be found on maps. The Gaelic for tree is *craobhe*. Occasionally the word is used together with the specific name of a tree, as in Achadh craobhe sgithich — the place of the hawthorn tree — a placename in Morvern. A wood or forest is *coille*, which is pronounced 'Killie' and spelt thus in the placename, Killiecrankie, in Perthshire. A woodman is *coilleair*. A thicket of trees is *bad* and a grove is *doire*, the former usually referring to a group of small trees, such as blackthorn, and the latter a group of large trees, such as oak, though *doire* may refer especially to a sacred grove, whether of oak or another type of tree. The usual word for a sapling is *fiuran*, but also *nearan* as in Cruach Nearan in Cowal. *Buinneag* is Gaelic for twig and *duileag* for leaf. The common word for nut is *chno* but *gruthair* is also used. I suspect that *chno* means specifically the nut of hazel, while *gruthair* means any kind of nut, probably including the acorn of the oak tree (*chno* is usually pronounced croe, as in Glencroe in Argyll). The timber of a tree, the material as cut for use, is *crann*. *Cairt* is Gaelic for bark and *freum* is a tree root. I have not attempted a full description of pronunciation for most of these words and the tree names, for pronunciation is so variable, as is spelling, between one area and another.

A geographical note: In spite of the so-called Highland Line it is difficult to define the exact extent of the area here referred to. Roughly speaking this book covers all the counties obviously Highland, plus the relevant parts of those that lie partly within the Highlands such as Dunbartonshire and Aberdeenshire. All the Hebridean Islands are included, plus Arran, and the Northern Isles — the Orkneys and the Shetlands. I have found it convenient, mainly because of historical references, to use old county names rather than District or Region or Island Authorities.

Inevitably there are gaps in the information provided. But there is enough here, with credit due to those acknowledged and in the list of references, to inspire and help others who have an interest in the life of trees which here in the Highlands of Scotland is displayed in great diversity and great beauty.

Hugh Fife
Crinan, Argyll
June 1994

Warriors and Guardians

Introduction

Picture a specific but not untypical Highland scene of the not so distant past — a township of a few families near the shore of a loch, on gentle ground at the foot of wooded hills. On the loch there are boats made of oak and pine, with oars and rudders of ash. Above the beach there are meadows hedged by hawthorn and holly. In the midst of the meadows are the houses with beams of oak and thatch supports of hazel, with furniture of elm and alder, and baskets of willow and bowls of elder. By the houses are rowans and there are cherry trees and blackthorns and elders for fruit. A river flows by the houses and there is a mill with a water-wheel of alder. Nearby are the osier-beds and along the banks are coppiced alders. The land rises to open pasture then to copses of hazel. Then there are oaks and huge ash trees, then pines and juniper on rocky knolls surrounded by seas of birch, rising high up the hills to the high crags where rowans grow. From those wild woods of oak and pine and elm and ash and birch and hazel and holly, the people in the township take timber and fuel, dyes, fertilisers and food.

They relied upon the trees and their way of life allowed for and demanded the indefinite flourishing of the trees. Extraction of timber was planned, rare trees encouraged and walls were built within the woods to allow for the benefits of winter grazing for sheep and cattle and for regeneration of trees.

Times change and certain requirements of natural and semi-natural woodland are now obsolete. The values of woodland to our predecessors were a part of a total lifestyle and a return to that lifestyle would mean the undoing of many worthwhile advances of recent years. The changes necessary to recreate the 'idyllic' landscape of the past would require the giving-up of too many social and economic gains of this century.

In a sense the great array of benefits allowed by a profusion of wild trees were no more than a compensation for the hardships and insecurities of an undeveloped society. For example, the abundant supply of fuel, free and ready-to-hand, available to a nineteenth century estate worker merely compensated for a ridiculously low wage. Yet how much has been lost, how fast and drastic the changes have been. We have a far greater range of materials available to us now, yet oak timber is an expensive luxury. We have a much more varied choice of foods, yet hazel nuts are costly.

Such conflict and contradictions are timeless — the argument in modern times, for instance, between the ecologist and the economist, between conserving and profit, may be only the latest version of man's unremitting need to come to terms with his place in the natural world.

Certainly it will be the impression of many people that the Highlands and Islands of Scotland is an area of stark beauty and barren majesty, where trees are too few to be of consequence to its attractions. At first glance, maps — even those that show plantations differently to natural woodland — appear to support this. But much forest land in the Highlands is on steep gradient and is shown only as narrow strips in two dimensions.

Indeed, many observers do not notice the extent of natural woodland because of the gradient — appearing as just a blur on a mountain slope, too rocky and remote to actually enter. Also, the word forest as seen on maps commonly refers to deer forest, most of which is virtually without trees.

But although it is true there are several million less trees than there were two centuries ago, there are in fact many parts where trees are the climax of the vegetation, and there are still sizeable forests of ancient origin. Native trees are more widespread and more varied than many people realise.

Such barrenness as is obvious is not the chief characteristic of the natural landscape. In the Scottish Highlands are the greatest oak-woods of North West Europe, and Britain's greatest birch-woods and alder-woods, and the oldest living tree in all Europe. Queen Victoria, who lived in the Highlands for a great part of each year — in the land she loved above all others in the world — frequently referred to the vast and beautiful woods in her travel journals. She loved the wild woods of the Scottish glens and was knowledgeable about the species she saw. Her frequent mention of woods in the Highland scenery — in a time when plantations of introduced species were few and far between — reveal the true nature of the glens.

The fantastic animal life of the Highlands would be of much less variety had there not been such a rich and varied tree cover now and in the past.

It is a tragic fact though, that there there has been a decline in the extent of wild forests and the animal life they support. Of course there have always been windswept islands, mountain peaks, moors and bogs, where trees will not grow, but the general landscape of the Highlands was very different not so very long ago.

Tree experts of the present day are able to discover which trees grew where in the past by analysing soil samples, for pollen from trees survives in the ground for a very long time. In the Highlands the history of trees can be dated back to the end of the last Ice Age, while in the south of England, beyond the limit of the Ice, their history can be dated several thousand years further back. By comparing different datings from different areas and comparing minute variations in pollen structure, experts have been able to understand parts of the evolution of the distinct types — discovering, bit by bit, how and where and when each type evolved from the primitive originals.

However, it is true to say that the general concept of a vast, unbroken Caledonian Forest is inaccurate and misleading. For a start, it was not something that disappeared in the remote, unknown past, for in the last two centuries it has declined as much as it did in the previous twenty centuries. Also it was not, as is commonly believed, a forest almost entirely of Scots pine. The decline of the Scots pine has been particularly highlighted and mourned, but this is because the Highlands is its only natural habitat. This significance has fortunately halted its decline, which is of benefit to its companion beasts and birds, but many other creatures that are especially associated with the Highlands are endangered because so many other tree types are considered of little importance.

The tree types studied in this book are all native to the region, or at least cannot reasonably be considered introduced. It is a little easier to ascertain which are locally native than it is in the south of Britain, as it is further from the woodlands of Southern Europe. During the few thousand years following the end of the last Ice Age, from about 10,000 BC until about 2,000 BC, trees spread north and west from mainland Europe and southern England. A few types came here from Northern Europe but most came, just as most migrating humans, from Central and Southern Europe by way of the 'land bridge' that still joined Britain to the continent.

A few types growing wild in the British Isles are of uncertain origin, and experts are unable to agree if a particular species is truly native or was introduced by man. One such type is hornbeam, another is box, but these do not grow wild in Scotland. Beech and sycamore are widespread, but both these have been introduced, beech perhaps from one of its few natural habitats in the south of England, and sycamore from Europe within the last three or four centuries. Such facts are known, and experts are reasonably certain which trees are native to Scotland and which are not, though there are exceptions. So trees such as beech and sycamore are not included in this book, nor are the various firs and spruces that are the common trees of large plantations. A few plantations comprise Scots pine but the 'Christmas tree' type of conifers are not native.

There are a few trees which cannot reasonably be termed native but yet just might possibly be so, notably whitebeam, crab-apple, white willow, sea-buckthorn and guelder rose. In such cases existing specimens just may have direct ancestry with trees that grew here naturally long ago, but there is no real evidence suggesting an existing natural spread, therefore these types are not included. (Although whitebeam is referred to in the chapter on the rowan tree.)

The order of the types dealt with here begins with those that are of slightly uncertain origin, that are rare, that have few practical uses, or little significance in folk-lore, or any combination of these points. There is also a general but not strict order of size from the smaller trees to the larger.

Rarity is, of course, a relative consideration — relative between area and area and between one type and another. Some of the trees studied here are naturally trees of solitude and not numerous, yet may be termed as wide-spread and common. Others are more numerous but are termed as rare, either because they are less common than elsewhere or less common than in the past. Some of the trees that tend naturally to solitude and isolation are in fact hardy and versatile and not as vulnerable to certain threats as the more widespread types.

Conservation and preservation of native trees is designated mostly by area rather than by species, thus trees that grow as forests, such as oak and pine, have greater status than the singular, or non-forest trees, such as rowan and elder. This situation is far from perfect, but blame does not lie with the organisations that own or manage the woodland reserves, like Scottish Natural Heritage and Forest Enterprise. They have to operate within the national structure as maintained by successive governments, a structure that envisages the nation as a collection of separate parts with specific functions — this area for industry, this for commerce, this for agriculture, this for recreation, this for conservation, and so on. Fortunately this is sometimes more theory than fact and those concerned with preservation, in spite of tight budgets, are slowly but surely making some headway. But the problems are vast, and while the pine and its dependent the osprey may have a fairly secure future, the hawthorn and the badger are still in decline.

The themes studied here are wide and varied and inter-related, yet they can be referred to under four basic headings. Each tree is looked at according to these aspects: **Laws of growth and regeneration; Companion beasts and plants; Practical uses; History, mythology and custom.**

The sources of the myths and legends used to illustrate this last theme are diverse and not exclusively of Highland origin. Some are universal. Many of the customs and beliefs included have been known in most parts of Britain and Ireland but it is a fact that the greatest diversity and persistence of customs belong to the areas that may still be called Celtic. One of the major sources of Celtic mythology used to convey this particular theme is the wide range of legend in the old annals and cycles of Ireland. During the so-called Dark Ages and following centuries the Irish Celts were among the most scholarly people in Europe. Yet in the Highlands and Islands of Scotland ancient traditions persisted with at least as much vigour and were still recognised in the nineteenth century, and thanks to certain writers much of the traditional lore was recorded before it all but died out.

It may be argued that ancient beliefs are best forgotten — at worst they are fearful superstitions surviving from pagan times when people were rough and uneducated; at best they are harmless fancies totally without relevance in the twentieth century. Yet they are synonymous with, or parallel to, the technical and scientific study of natural history, without which the twenty-first century cannot be planned for. However far man's technological brilliance advances the strengths and the weaknesses of nature are always bound to affect us.

In the past general knowledge about trees was far more widespread than now. It is likely that the most knowledgeable persons knew many of the facts that are only now being discovered through modern science. The impression that our ancestors of long ago tore nearly all the forest from the land and quite suddenly most of the country became grassland does not make sense within the real scale of time. Agriculture grew quite rapidly in importance but the removal of large areas of woodland took place over centuries and centuries. No particular race, tribe or culture intended a complete change in the natural ground cover of the land, for the products of an abundant tree life meant not only fuel and wild foods but the timber that was essential for successful agriculture. People respected the trees and parallel to their need for woodland products was their worship of trees as symbols of their spiritual needs and doctrines. This book illustrates how customs and rituals were born from observation and practical needs, yet also that worship of nature was not totally the result of superstition and fear of hunger.

Some of our ancestors' customs, rituals and superstitions certainly were born of fear and of ignorance, yet many had direct benefits and others were in pure celebration of those benefits. The emphasis has always been shifting. The complexity and significance of tree lore has not remained constant. Thus in one place a priest was bowing down before a yew while in another a woodman was felling a rowan; and a century later the priest was no more and a farmer was felling the poisonous yew to protect his livestock, while in the other place another woodman was bowing down before a rowan. So in time and geography there is no expansive lore of trees, no 'universal' all-important complexity of beliefs.

But nevertheless it was usual for Highland people to recognise tree lore more or less throughout history, from the earliest wanderers to the crofters and estate workers of the last century. It was usual to observe seasonal festivals using fires of particular wood, to avoid harming certain trees, and it was usual to learn proverbs, poems and tales relating to the trees.

At certain times in history, particularly more remote times, the significance of trees was an important part of a complex code of living, an all-embracing cosmology. The wise taught that the trees symbolised order and balance, and they imitated the character of particular trees in their rituals, presumably to show their god, goddess or whatever their awareness and gratefulness.

So tree lore has been important to both land-workers and to holy men, but it has also had a place in leadership and governing — from the sacrificial death of the king on a fire of oak long, long ago, to the willow rod of the Lords of the Isles, and to the planting of ash and yew by more recent lairds. In fact to some extent particular types, classes or roles of people had particular systems of tree lore, even relating especially to one kind of tree. It is almost certainly impossible to discover if there ever was a comprehensive symbolism of this kind.

Many kinds of tree represented many trades, positions and classes and surviving tradition reveals that there has been a fairly wide connecting of pine with warrior, hazel with priest or priestess, oak with king. And trees have specific human characteristics, motives and emotions, such as alder for secretiveness, willow for health, birch for love. Specific trees were even considered especially male or especially female. Most definitely female were rowan, hawthorn and holly, and most definitely male were alder, pine and oak.

Such kinds of symbolism, like all forms of tree lore, can be traced to the factual uses and observable features of the trees, but sometimes the connections are vague and the characterisation verges on the imaginative and purest fancy of story-telling. For in the stories trees become something beyond their habitats, their uses and their human-like characteristics. They become the symbols of desires that are not earthly, of enchantments and spiritual goals, of magical spirits and gods and goddesses, of ancient yearnings for a Celtic paradise.

And what of the future? Perhaps paradoxically, this work tries to show how lovely, how rich and how varied are the woodlands of the Highlands yet also how sad, depleted and vulnerable. If the remaining trees are but a glimpse of long-gone forest of enormous area then the wide bare tracts of the Highlands of today are a glimpse of the future, when native trees growing wild are eradi-cated entirely, as wild flowers are from fields of modern-day agriculture. This, of course, is not likely to happen while there can be special reserves, but it seems only right and proper that there should be a certain abundance and variety of native trees in all areas except those where nature denies them.

Being 'right and proper' means that the advantages outweigh the disadvantages, that the need for conserving and encouraging has a cause and result more important than individual designs that are or would be hampered by such a policy. The basis of this need is perhaps consid-eration for the continuity of the trees and their dependents regardless of our own existence, though this reason alone is weak and many would deplore it.

Man, like all other living things, cannot thrive without harming and exploiting other forms of life. Were we to take conservation to an extreme we would doom ourselves to extinction, and this in turn, in spite of our often destructive ways, would not wholly benefit other living things. And it would be unreasonable for one of us to expect another to live in extreme hardship in order to maintain the principle of conservation.

Yet there are many ways, some so small and simple, in which we could adapt the processes of our existence to allow for realistic conservation. There are surely compromises available that would lead to the end of the fears felt by certain people in certain circumstances — fears of total conservation or fears of a total destruction. Within any compromise there must be a commercial validity. Even supposing that many of the trees' traditional products are and will remain unnecessary and replaceable with other materials, there are yet as many and more that are important now and in the future.

For even though the imagery of the trees is largely faded now, even though their everyday importance has greatly lessened, and even though their numbers have so dwindled, they are still here to be seen for what they are and in great numbers. There are millions of wild trees growing in the Highlands, young and old, dense and scattered, broadleaf and evergreen, rare and common, and every one enriches us all.

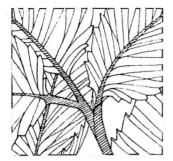

Elder

The elder tree is known by many names. It is the bour tree and the stinking tree, and in Gaelic it is *ruis* and occasionally *dromain*. It is often termed a shrub, for it has a spreading, irregular form and usually reaches only about 12 feet in height. But some may be twice this and have a straighter, wider trunk.

It is rare in the strongholds of Gaelic and placenames using the word *ruis* are few — possible examples are Craigruie in Perthshire, Glenrisdell in Kintyre, Strath Rusdale in Easter Ross, and Ben Ruisg, Dunbartonshire.

The word *dromain* is given in some translations for the alder, an alternative to the more usual *fearn*, but one clue to the original meaning is the Gaelic word *dromanach*, which is a small peg once used for securing thatch and which was commonly made of elder wood. One placename using the word *dromain* is Barrach-an-dromain, on the island of Mull.

The elder is almost certainly native to most of the Southern Hebrides that are close to the mainland, and is otherwise scattered throughout the southern Highlands and parts of the east, being most common in Mid-Argyll, Cowal, Stirlingshire, Dunbartonshire, Banffshire, Morayshire and Nairnshire.

The elder is in some ways particular about the conditions it requires, while in other ways it is remarkably adaptable. It does like fairly deep, well-drained soil, and

There must surely be some connection between the belief that an elder by the house or by the garden gate would keep malignant spirits away and the fact that its leaves deter most flies.

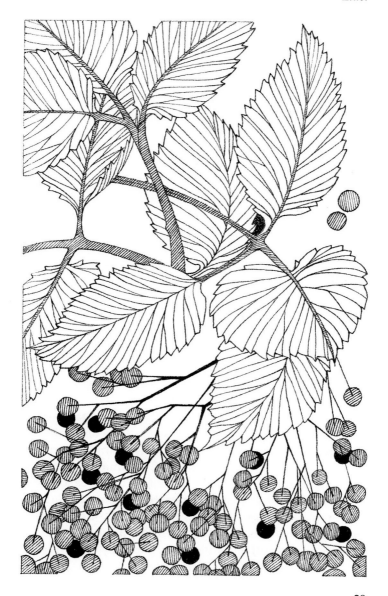

it dislikes both excessive light and deep shade. But it will thrive where other trees may not and is resistant to polluted air and soil. In fact it has been observed that it likes to grow in or near refuse and rotting waste, and because it likes, or at least tolerates, the presence of rotting animal remains it has sometimes been accorded the character of a malignant parasite. The Saxons avoided the elder, believing that it could only grow where human blood had been spilt.

In contrast to this the elder has commonly been valued for its beauty. In early summer, from late June until late July, it is at its prettiest, being covered in domed clusters of tiny cream-white flowers which have a very pleasant, sweet scent. In the autumn, usually by mid-September, the tiny berries which have replaced the bi-sexual flowers have turned to dark purple-black. Both these features are a part of the tree's ornamental value and both can be harvested as welcome products, the flowers for flavouring jams and for refreshing drinks and the berries for the famous wine and for sauces, jelly and puddings. Some people find the fruits too astringent or sharp for eating straight from the tree, but others would disagree.

The tree's general form — its spread crown, compact size, the curve of its fissured trunk and the vitality of its pale grey/orange shoots and suckers — is also relevant to its role in parks and gardens as an ornamental tree. In spite of, and in a sense because of, its small stature, the varied colours make it easily identified in all seasons and all locations. In late January or early February the orange and grey of its twigs and bark is tinged by the bright green of its opening buds. The young leaves, appearing earlier than those of all other native trees, then stay in seemingly suspended growth until about mid-April, when the stems with single leaf and two or three pairs renew their advance. When there is a severe late frost the young leaves may suffer, though this does not affect the flowering and fruiting. In traditional country lore the opening of the elder flowers is taken as the signal for seed-sowing in the fields.

The elder has the unkind alternative name of 'stinking tree' because of the unpleasant smell of its leaves. The smell keeps certain insects that may be damaging to the tree at a distance and deters most birds that might like to eat its berries. However bees and hoverflies are not put off, and by feeding on the blossoms they assist fertilisation. And certain birds such as robins and pigeons eat the berries and thus assist in the dispersal of the seeds. Even after a poor summer the elder produces an abundance of fruit, yet its continuity in the Highlands is, for various reasons, under threat.

Suitable conditions of soil and climate are few and far between, and a thriving seedling has little chance of surviving the presence of beasts that graze or browse. And these days man usually treats the elder as a weed, caring little for its beauty or its fruits. There are few craftsmen still using its timber. These days many are cleared away with power-saws and left to rot, whereas in the past the continuity of the elder was considered important to many aspects of rural life.

Apart from its appearance, and apart from the value of its fruit, craftsmen had many uses for its trunk and stems. The stems have a soft, pithy centre and are easily hollowed and then fashioned into tubes for bellows and for various musical instruments. The hard wood of the main trunk has long been valued for a variety of household artefacts, most especially bowls and spoons and forks. The Travelling Families of Scotland were well-known for their skill in making spoons and forks of elder wood, and probably they also made most of the pegs, the *dromanach*, used by house-dwellers for securing thatch. Makers of dye also sought elder trees, using leaves and bark and even berries in their craft. And herbalists, or village spey-wives, gathered the berries for a variety of medicinal concoctions, including skin ointment and a drink to soothe sore throats.

There are many customs and superstitions associated with the elder, all of which have some basis in accurate observation and have some practical merit. There was once a taboo against it for firewood. This was partly in consideration of its supposed magical qualities but also showed consideration for its rarity (besides which it is not that good as a fuel anyway!). There must surely be some connection between the belief that an elder by the house or by the garden gate would keep malignant spirits away and the fact that its leaves deter most flies. Perhaps our ancestors planted them by their windows and doors for the same reason we hang chemical sticks in our houses today — to keep germ-carrying insects, 'malignant spirits', away from habitations.

Even today there are some country people that retain the old custom of wearing elder leaves in the hair or clothing when out walking or working. It has been believed that the elder contains within it, or is presided over by, a spirit or spirits of benign nature, and that it is this feature of the tree that wards off evil or mischievous beings.

To please the spirit of the tree, to secure its protection or to repay it for the products it provides, people used to leave offerings of cakes and milk in its shade. If the fairies that dwelt there didn't get them first then the creatures that lived in the vicinity must have welcomed these tasty additions to their usual diet. Badgers, for instance, favour the vicinity of elders and eat the berries that fall. The seeds pass through them intact and thus the badger assists the elder in propogation.

The elder has strong associations with religion and mystical beings. Its small size for a tree means it is often referred to as a shrub. In folklore this is explained by the belief that the Crucifixion cross was made of elder wood, as remembered in the old saying from central Scotland, "Ever bush and never tree, since our Lord was nailed t'ye." How this belief originated is difficult to know. It was by no means the only kind of wood that was associated with the cross.

In whatever way it may have been incorporated into localised Christian tradition, there is no doubt that the elder had a part in older spiritual symbolism. It has many similarities in its mythological role to the rowan tree, having been considered to be especially dear to beings that were only partly manifest in our world, and having fruits and flowers and twigs that could lay enchantment on ordinary mortals.

The folklore and superstition connected with elders is not of course exclusively of Highland origin. The customs and taboos, and the symbolic stories that have characterised them, are known in Brittany, Cornwall, Wales and the Isle of Man, yet since its relatively recent colonisation of the Highlands (perhaps within the last two thousand years) it has been accorded a special status here.

How unfortunate then, if they are not allowed to thrive and must depend only upon the suckers that shoot from the roots in order to spread. Badgers and other beasts and birds are not always numerous enough to ensure constant seed dispersal. The ecology of its habitats is changing and such seeds that begin to germinate find it increasingly harder to thrive. Now few craftsmen are left to protect and encourage it and in parks and gardens its place is now being taken by introduced trees and shrubs. It is not in imminent danger of Highland extinction but the elder's future is not secure.

Warriors and Guardians

Cherry

Both kinds of native British cherry trees are found growing wild in the Highlands. These are the wild cherry or gean, and the bird cherry. (Some experts believe that the latter is not truly native here.) Bird cherry is in fact quite common in parts of the Highlands and is undoubtedly a true native, whereas the wild cherry is commonly found around habitations and its natural distribution is much masked by planting, and many that are found in the wild are likely to be the offspring of planted specimens. They have been planted mainly for ornamental reasons, in parks, gardens, on the borders of conifer plantations and in past centuries, close to farmhouses. But this practice is no longer very common, now that there are many imported and hybrid forms to choose from. (Offspring of hybrid forms with close relation to the native wild originals may revert to that form.)

Those specimens that are found close to planted cherries, that can be assumed to be the offspring of the planted trees, will probably have grown from seeds dropped by birds that eat the fruits, such as robins, thrushes, blackbirds and finches, unless they are close to the parent tree, in which case they may be suckers.

While there are many similarities between the gean and the bird cherry, there are also some notable differences.

The bird cherry reaches about 20 feet, occasionally quite a bit more, and it has a fairly smooth dark reddish-brown bark. The emerald green leaves, opening in late April, are finely-toothed, and they are wider and less spear-shaped than other forms of cherry. The bi-sexual flowers are very small but can be numerous and dense, the clusters of white blooms on slender stems growing in abundance on every twig. They usually open shortly after the leaf-buds, although the flowering time of this tree varies more than most — anything from early May to mid-June. Pollination is by insects, though the tree is generally self-sterile. The small black fruits are ripe by late July or early August.

Although many birds eat the fruits and disperse the seeds, the odds against any one seed developing into a mature tree are enormous and its habit of reproducing by sucker is vital to its propagation. The new trees growing by sucker from the roots of the parents maintain a habitat where seeds are not creating renewal and also help to overcome the limitations created by the tree's usually self-sterile conditions, for their flowers can fertilise — and be fertilised by — the parent tree, so increasing the production of fruits. Among the factors that can limit successful sucker propagation is lack of light. This will also affect propagation by seed, as will exposure to strong winds, and the presence of grazing or browsing creatures. The strength of sucker growth can actually increase if the parent tree is cut down or falls.

The tree is hardy to acid soils but is fussy of its position in relation to other plants, land-formation and weather conditions. It favours the presence of woodland but not the depths of woodland. It tolerates the cold of high altitude but not exposure to strong winds. It is moisture-loving but will not tolerate water-logging.

It finds its ideal in many parts of the Highlands, in localised habitats scattered here and there. Its favoured range seems to be across the Central Highlands in a slight diagonal from Northern Argyll to the counties around the Moray Firth, with its greatest density being close to Loch Ness. At Drumnadrochit, about halfway up the northern shore of that loch, there is a profusion of bird cherry. Here the conditions are ideal, where there is a steady but slow flow and spread of water off the high hills.

The wild cherry, or gean, has a similar range of spread, though with a slightly greater dominance towards the north and north-east (more common in such parts than bird cherry even though it is the bird cherry that is more northern in Britain as a whole).

It has similar processes of propagation, though slightly more by seed and slightly less by sucker. In general it is more tolerant of exposure, in fact actually favouring habitats where competing plants are few and small. It is tolerant of frost and its seeds (as do the seeds of bird cherry) actually require chilling before they will germinate. The seeds are borne in red fruits, like the red fruits of cultivated cherries for harvest though slightly smaller. Many birds, virtually as many as for bird cherry, eat the fruits and thus aid dispersal of seed. Thereafter their development is beset by a number of threats and difficulties.

The soil must be not too acid and fairly rich in nutrients. There must be reasonable light and reasonable drainage. There must be a lack of grazing and browsing creatures, such as rabbits, sheep and deer. In spite of these particular requirements and the need for reasonable frosts to promote germination before the seeds start to rot or are eaten by creatures of the soil, the gean is found in some surprisingly unlikely settings.

It is a feature of certain of the smaller and rarer trees of the Highlands that they may thrive in conditions very different from those that are described as ideal in most books on trees. Such descriptions are generally based upon observation of habitats in the south of Britain, while in northern Scotland the gean survives partly by long-term adaptation to harsher conditions and also by taking advantage of areas where there are few other large plants to compete with for light and such nutrition as might be found. Thus, though in the south of Britain it is a tree of woodland or woodland edges, in the Highlands it is more common away from the well wooded regions. Basically it favours compromise, doing best in the regions between the more fertile parts and the colder, more exposed and barren areas.

Typically it will choose a hillside, not too high up and

not too low down, a slope of averagely wet ground where the soil is adequately rich but simple, where a few other trees grow here and there. It may choose a spot on the edge of a copse of small birch, benefiting from their leaf-mould and by their shelter while reaching out toward the open. In such a situation they grow to about 20 feet in height — their maximum is quite a bit more but wild specimens in the Highlands rarely exceed this, especially those that grow in the wildest and most unlikely places.

Yet in spite of their tendency to settings where conditions are not of a very mild and tame nature they strive to grow in a regular shape. The trunk is generally one to three feet in diameter, maintaining a regular thickness from roots to where the branches reach out, usually about four to eight feet up. The bark is a greyish-brown and smooth, peeling here and there on mature specimens to reveal a reddishness. The branches are upreaching and slender. The spear-shaped leaves, a little longer than those of bird cherry, are a bright green and finely-toothed, and they do not open until late April but mature rapidly. In autumn they turn a pleasant shade of orange. The clusters of little white flowers on long slender stems appear about the same time. They are bi-sexual but like those of the bird cherry, they can only pollinate and be pollinated by, the flowers of another tree.

The disadvantage this creates is offset to some extent by the production of suckers. But sucker growth is weaker than that of bird cherry and the gean often stands alone. The actual habitats of the gean are more common than those of bird cherry but its numbers are less.

Its favoured habitats and its sporadic spread both geographically and in time, are a part of its rather special place in Gaelic folklore, a place of greater significance than the bird cherry. The following description of the cherry's part in Highland folklore refers almost specifically to the gean — there is not much to be said specifically of the bird cherry in this case, although we can assume that it shared at least some of the gean's characteristics.

In Gaelic the wild cherry is often called *fhioghag*, which literally means fig. I am not sure why it should be called a fig tree. Perhaps there is a Biblical connection or perhaps it is a fairly recent name, given to the tree by Highland seamen returning from the Mediterranean. Either way *fhioghag* is probably not a very ancient name for the tree, and the alternative Gaelic name *cacothaich* is almost certainly of greater antiquity.

The nature of the gean's growth has given it a rather mystical character. Growing singly, or virtually so — sometimes in high isolated glens and ravines, sometimes on cliffs and promontories, sometimes alone among birch or oak — and its transient nature, appearing and disappearing, as well as its beauty, has created its magical image in Highland tales and customs. Its discovery had meaning, as a herald of fate, either good or bad, and it was surrounded with superstition, so that it was taboo to exploit the tree in all but a very few ways. Many Gaels would not use its wood either for products or for fuel, and they would not eat its fruits. Taking fruits or suckers for planting near the home was acceptable and sometimes the fruits were fed to cattle to cure stomach ailments. Nevertheless few taboos associated with this or any other tree have had continuous recognition over a long period of time and over wide regions.

A superstition will have meant less in one area than another, or it will be forgotten in one area sooner, or indeed it may have grown in importance having been more subtle and less demanding longer ago.

Thus the taboos relating to cherry trees have not meant that there is no tradition of their practical use. The hardness of the wood and its fine, attractive grain have not been unexploited, and it has been used for bowls, for furniture and for ornaments. The wild cherry, the gean, is the direct ancestor of the present cultivated cherry of the orchards in the south of England, and every now and again — when the Highland summer has been especially good — the fruit of our wild cherries ripens to delicious perfection. In this it has an importance, as well as an attraction in a garden, a park, by a road or a forestry plantation.

It has a value in the wild to us, to insects and to birds, and it has a special place in country lore, not least in its most favoured Highland habitats, such as Lochaber, Western Angus, Moray and Easter Ross.

It is probable that its spread here has halved within the last two centuries. Although it has never been extremely widespread, and it is one of the 'newer' trees, having arrived two to three thousand years ago, it has established itself well and manages to thrive in some unlikely and relatively safe places. Its cousin, the bird cherry, is much the same, with similar background, spread and prospects. It seems right to hope that the strengths of these beautiful trees will give them a secure future. The merest attentions to their needs, just slight recognition of their situation, would aid that security, perhaps enable them to expand their domains again.

Yew

Among all the native Highland trees considered in this book, the rarest is the yew. Though Europe's largest yew woods are in fact in England, it is rare in the British Isles as a whole. The chances of finding a truly wild yew in the Highlands are extremely slight.

A description of its growth and distribution is little more than a historical account but because of its historical significance and positive long-term existence in the Scottish Highlands it does merit inclusion. The relatively wide distribution of planted specimens is not at all unrelated to its natural, ancient status, not least because it is extremely long-lived, longer than any other native tree. It often exceeds a thousand years. And in fact the oldest living thing in all Europe — a yew reckoned to be four thousand years old — is here in the Highlands.

Identification of the yew is quite simple. The type of yew native to the Highlands is the English yew which, with few exceptions, is the principal type found right across Europe and Western Asia. One such exception is the Irish yew, which is very localised as a wild tree though commonly planted in other parts of the British Isles. The yew is an evergreen but experts are cautious when listing it as a conifer. Unlike the holly, which is evergreen yet certainly not coniferous, it has needles rather than leaves, (or more precisely needle-type foliage). Yet it does not bear cones but soft fruits. If they are not in any obvious

The special religious symbolism of the yew lies in its immortality and eternity

way like cones they are still not easily classified and add to the general difficulties of putting the yew into any particular category. So it is either an evergreen deciduous, an individual form of conifer, or more or less unique, although the juniper is in some ways similar.

Basically, a tree is a tree and any one specific type is not, in terms of evolution, totally unrelated to all the others and the yew actually represents the link between conifers and deciduous trees. This is most apparent in its foliage, for the needles are soft and flat and veined, showing that true needles and true leaves share evolutionary origins.

Whatever its status — coniferous, deciduous or unique — it is certainly a tree of peculiarities, of unique features that are as enigmatic and mysterious as its ancient role in mythology and legend, yet which positively aid identification. The fruit it produces for instance, is very distinctive and individual. It is more or less round, in fact slightly oval, a dull pinkish red, and open at the end revealing a green inside. No other fruit is really comparable, though I cannot resist likening it to a stuffed olive with the colours reversed! Such trunk as is visible below the dense foliage is rusty brown, very rough and ridged on mature specimens and sometimes several feet across. The many branches reach outward then curve upward, and may reach a height above ground of 60 feet, though such a height is unusual. The tiny flowers are borne on separate trees though occasionally together, and the male are the more conspicuous, sometimes producing great quantities of golden pollen.

On the whole flowering and fruiting are irregular and with each fruit containing just one seed, reproduction is not vigorous. Pollination having taken place, successful germination of seeds is infrequent and when it does occur special requirements and specific threats can work against successful growth of the seedlings. The tree's long life can compensate the low level of fruiting to some extent but this in turn is counteracted by the slow growth of seedling trees. While small, they are very vulnerable to damage. The damage may be done by weather conditions, such as severe frost or flooding, by parasite growths and insects, by grazing beasts and by trampling from beasts and even man.

The special requirements that limit natural propogation are many and subtle. Acid soil, thin soil, long spells of cold and damp, frequent strong winds — all these factors, in various combinations, can prohibit the spread of the yew.

Its natural distribution in the Highlands is impossible to verify. Certainly it is naturally very rare and probably always has been. Nevertheless it is known that it has grown here for thousands of years and it is very likely that only in recent times has it declined from rare to virtually extinct as a wild tree. The fact that its foliage is poisonous to most farm animals has undoubtedly meant that man has often felled and burned it and this practice will have been most common in the last century or two when livestock farming largely replaced cultivation.

The shoots of young seedlings are hardly poisonous at all, particularly to sheep. But unfortunately for both the tree and the animals themselves, domesticated beasts do not have the best instincts for what is edible and what is not. The fruits, contrary to common belief, are not poisonous and a number of wild creatures eat them, notably foxes, badgers, thrushes, blackbirds and redwings. While not potentially fatal like the foliage, the fruits are not absolutely safe for human consumption. The seed is not digested and thus these creatures can aid dispersal. Unfortunately the seed takes up to 18 months to germinate, during which time it has to withstand the dangers of extreme weather conditions. So with one thing and another the yew is very endangered as a wild plant of the Highlands.

Its natural distribution, or what it might have been more than a couple of centuries ago, is principally the southern Highlands, particularly Argyll, Dunbartonshire, Perthshire and the North-East Highlands, in parts of Morayshire, Banffshire and north-east Inverness-shire — the land of the Clan Fraser, whose clan badge was a sprig of yew. In these places existing yew trees mostly reflect a long-term spread but ancient distribution can, to some extent, be guesssed at by a study of placenames.

A look at placenames is slightly complicated by the fact that the more common and similar tree, juniper, is often called the mountain yew and it is likely that some of the placenames using the Gaelic word for yew — *iubhair* or *euair* — actually refer to the juniper. Examples of placenames which may or may not refer to the yew are Craignure on Mull, Eurach on the Argyll mainland, and Tomnahurrich in Inverness. There is another rarer word for yew, *togh* and this may be the origin of the name Auchtoo in Perthshire. But there are placenames using the more common word that almost certainly refer to the yew rather than mountain yew, notably Iona and Kilneuair, again in Argyll. It is virtually certain that these places of religion have an ancient affinity with the yew, or it with them, and the origins of this affinity might well prove that the present distribution is directly related to an ancient and totally natural distribution rather than having been introduced.

It is generally held that the name Iona stems in part from the holy island's earlier name, which was Ioua. This was the old Pictish or Pictish/Gaelic word for the yew and was almost certainly connected with the pre-Christian cult of the yew as observed on the island. The yew cult, as a form of Druidism, was absorbed into the growth of Christianity on Iona in the fifth or sixth century. The Iona Church then spread to the mainland and one of the first churches founded was Kilneuair, near Loch Awe. This was probably 'the church of the yew', though it may have been 'the church of Ioua'. Either way this church (now a ruin but not extremely so, having remained very important for many centuries) had connections with the religious significance of the tree, both Druidic and Christian.

The special religious symbolism of the yew lies in its immortality and eternity, symbolised by it being evergreen and by its slow and long-lasting growth, and probably in part related to rarity, individuality and general 'air of mystery'. Such features were observed by Christians, Druids and the priests of even older religions, and thus yews were planted in holy places.

It may seem that this indicates that the present distribution of yews and of placenames referring to yews has little or no relation to a natural spread, but this is not the case. For it may well be that it was not always the practice to bring the yew to a place of sanctity but rather the reverse.

Take, for instance, the 4,000 year old yew of Fortingall, near Loch Tay. The church and graveyard are very much younger, and in the creation of a Christian site the previous existence of a religious structure used by the Caledonians made it likely that for priests, or people in general, the tree **was** the religious structure.

One can imagine the finding of this yew, perhaps by a lone wanderer or perhaps by a migrating tribe — the strangeness of the tree, or at least its unexpected finding, perhaps in winter, then glad recognition or gradual growing of reverence and respect. Then later the building of a church and the creation of a graveyard, visits by tree experts to analyse the yew's age, and by sightseers. All this relating directly to its origins is of course only supposition, for it may have been planted, like others since. But somehow there are just too many places with affinity to the yew in the Highlands, too long an association, too deep a tradition, for it to be very unlikely that the present distribution of yews, including those most obviously planted, and of placenames, has a direct connection with an ancient and totally natural distribution.

Through Christian symbolism, through the cult of the yew and also through historical reference to use of the tree's timber — in the study of these can be seen the age-old importance of the yew in the Highlands. The extreme rarity of the tree, its naturally thin spread even in the past, might suggest that practical use of its timber was traditionally restricted. But there is little evidence of this. It is likely that it was taboo to use the wood as fuel, protecting its existence and also in observation of its religious significance, but the timber has had special uses apparently without any limiting taboos. Uses such as furniture making, utilising its deep colour and fine grain, have presumably been practised throughout history just as the wood is still valued today. But it is perhaps in the making of weapons that the apparent lack of taboos is most surprising.

It is known that weapons for hunting and for war were

made from yew thousands of years ago, for the wood is very slow to rot and in certain locations, for instance in peat and in blocked caves, archaeologists have found weapons of such an age. These finds have been chiefly of spears and small bows, but it is in more recent history that the yew as a weapon gained special distinction. It is well known that the famous English and Welsh archers of battles such as Agincourt in 1415 used longbows of yew, the strength and pliancy of the wood being unmatched by any other. It is less well known, yet just as certain, that the Scottish archers used yew long-bows in Bruce's victory over the English at Bannockburn in 1314. It is said that the king, when rallying support in Argyll, came to Ardchattan priory and ordered long-bows to be made from the sacred yews there.

There is no evidence that this act, nor any similar, provoked anger in religious circles, or in the people whose ancestors were buried under the yews. Perhaps this was one use of the tree's timber that was actually endorsed by the religious tradition, perhaps in some strange way drawing a connection between a weapon to kill and the tree's ritual and symbolic associations with death.

We know that Bruce's long-bows (or most of them) came from the yews of Ardchattan, and we know that most of the archers at Bannockburn were under the Lord of the Isles, and that warriors of the Highlands before and since used bows of yew. Thus the regions where the yew had a very strong religious significance also had a tradition of yew wood weapons. There is an old Gaelic poem which translates,

Bow of the yew of Easragan,
Silk of Gall vinn,
Arrow of the birch of Doire-Donn,
Feather of the eagle of Loch Treig.

Just how widespread and important the so-called cult of the yew was is not easily guessed. It is known that it was once common practice to bury a piece of yew with the dead, and the Druids used a stave of yew wood with notches or runes to record phases of the moon and / or their traditional laws. It is likely that the yew cult as such was really just an element of a wider religion, a religion incorporating a great many features of the natural environment as mystical symbols.

Christianity, particularly the early Celtic Church, also recognised the tree as a symbol of immortality, eternity and the greater mysteries of life and death. From the earliest days of its worship, even before the Druids, through the many forms of Christianity, right up until the present day, the yew has retained a special importance in the Highlands — as a symbol of spiritual belief, as a weapon, as a timber for things of beauty, as a grand sentinel at the gateways of estates and gardens. In all these ways (and of course as a food supply for badgers, thrushes and other creatures) it has had and still has a role to play. What a loss then, if it is no longer to be a truly wild tree in the Highlands. Perhaps we can give it a helping hand in some small way to ensure that it can have a future.

Aspen

The little aspen, rarely exceeding 25 feet, is the smallest of all poplars, and the only poplar native to northern Britain. Its tendency is to grow in solitude, rarely close to many others of its kind or to other trees, but it is hardy and though in Britain as a whole it is most common in the gentle country of the south west, in the Highlands it is most common in the north west and the islands.

It's usual Gaelic name is *crithean*, as in Blarcreen in Appin and Sron a crithean in Ardgower. It has also been called *eagh*, as in Eagach in Glencoe, and perhaps Eigheach in Perthshire. Areas where it is relatively easy to find include Sutherland, Speyside, Wester Ross, The Outer Isles, the Great Glen and the islands of Iona, Colonsay and Skye.

Its usual habitat is steep rock-faces, sometimes by the sea and sometimes on inland mountains, and here its resilience allows it to thrive out of reach of grazing and browsing animals. Thus, even though there are wide areas where aspens are not found, it maintains its presence in most of the Highland counties.

The thinkers and observers in our history drew the aspen into the lore and customs of their culture with this consideration. The attractive little aspen 'roamed' the hills and islands in its almost secretive way, its virtually invisible seeds taken by roaming winds — a million seeds going without trace while just one produces a 'sudden' tree from its landing place in a crack of a cliff. The pattern of its distribution, both geographically and in time, was symbolised by the unexpected discovery of an individual or small group by the wanderers of legend and myth. The discovery held a particular meaning. It was an omen, even if not necessarily a good one. The part the aspen plays in mythology is presumably very ancient, and like some other rare trees its character has gone through changes. Fantasy becomes superstition, and vice versa.

At some stage since the arrival of Christianity in the Highlands, recognition of the tree became a fear, or at least a dislike. What may have been a storyteller's imaginative expansion became the belief that wood of aspen was used for the Crucifixion cross. This was believed of other trees, and was probably of imaginative origin. It is possible that such ideas were introduced by Christian missionaries who wished to discredit trees that were worshipped. If so, then the belief is relatively recent for within the original Highland Christianity such forms of nature worship were not generally discouraged.

Before this, in pre-Christian times, the aspen was probably better liked and may have had a special magic akin to the rowan. Even until recently it was believed that sound of wind through its quaking leaves induced prophetic insight. Yet again the origins of its most feared character may pre-date Christianity and have something to do with a specific, long forgotten event. And the Gaelic saying, "Malison be on thee, O aspen cursed, on thee was crucified the king of kings", may have had a version of similar sentiment in pre-Christian times.

The opinions, from different eras, and different places, cursing the aspen or praising it, have meant that it has had few traditional, down-to-earth, uses. There has been a strong taboo in the Highlands against using it for anything to do with fishing or farming, and it was considered absolute taboo to use its timber in house construction. Whether this began with respect or superstitious fears has helped to save a tree of naturally sparce distribution from possible extinction. In its own subtle way it is an important part of Highland ecology, and in its own enigmatic way it is a part of the beauty and the romantic tradition of the land. Its survival here has to some extent been aided by its popularity with some gardeners and landscapers, the main reason for which is its foliage.

The pretty leaves are on fine, supple stems and the slightest breeze sets them fluttering — hence its botanical name *populus tremula* (trembling poplar). They create a distinctive sound, the sound that inspired seers, and that was referred to by Highland men bemoaning the incessant chatter and nagging of their wives!

Adding to the attraction of the tree's appearance in early summer are the silvery catkins, the male of which are red beneath the fine hairs and the female of which are blue. The two sexes are never on the same tree, a fact which contributes to the tree's scarcity. Pollen is transferred by wind, like the seeds, and although various insects feed on parts of the tree, pollen is not carried by insects. Seedlings like heathery country and orchids are a common companion plant in many of its habitats.

Aspens are almost certainly rarer than they should be in the Highlands but the distribution is naturally thin. Just how endangered the species is will not be known until yet more is known about the natural history of its native regions.

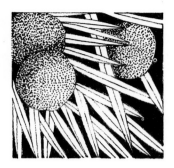

Juniper

The common juniper, the single form that is native to the Highlands, is usually very small and dense, appearing more like a bush of gorse than a tree. It is however, usually termed a tree because of its systems of regeneration and growth and its 'family connections'. Some individuals are indeed of towering form like the yew tree. And like the yew it is an evergreen but not a conifer in the usual sense.

In fact the juniper is sometimes called the mountain yew and some placenames incorporating the Gaelic word for yew, *iubhair*, actually refer to the presence of the juniper (see the chapter on the yew tree). Other Gaelic names for the juniper are *aittin* and *samh*, as in the placenames Attadale in Wester Ross and the island of Samhan, near Mull.

Juniper is a common tree in the Highlands but it does not have a wide distribution. It is most common on the coasts and islands of the mid-west and in Braemar and other southern parts of the Grampians, in the deep glens of Inverness-shire where there are, or have been, big forests of Scots pine, and in parts of Sutherland, Caithness, Moray and Nairn — in which places the clans of Ross, Murray and Gunn adopted the juniper as their clan badge. Although it favours the hillsides and moorlands that are or have been the habitat of Scots pine it can also thrive on near-barren cliffs and shores. In such habitats it thrives because of the lack of competition from larger plants. Considering its companionship with pine, this is a bit of a paradox but the story of the juniper is full of such contradictions. Just why it should be rare in the south-west Highlands yet even here be locally common, for example on the mainland coasts facing Jura, is not easily understood.

The story of the juniper is very, very old and its changing fortunes are almost beyond a time scale we can properly comprehend. Very soon after the ice receded, some 10,000 years ago, the juniper began to colonise the tundra lands of northern Britain, one of the first trees to do so, certainly the first in the higher country. At one time, perhaps about 5,000 years ago, it was numerous all over the Highlands. Then, because of climatic changes, but most particularly because of the advance of other large plants, it began to decline, though only very gradually. This decline is natural, unaided by man, but now we are turning that decline into a straight fall and the future of the juniper is not healthy.

The rarity of young ones today is in one sense surprising, considering the hardiness of the tree and its methods of regeneration. Unlike most other trees its flowers can be pollinated by either insects or wind. It fruits are eaten by many creatures, such as mice and other rodents and many kinds of bird, particularly the crested tit. The seeds pass through undigested and are thus spread far and wide. The seeds are likely to fall on ground that is suitable for their germination but thereafter the seedlings are vulnerable to grazing beasts. Apart from the sudden increase of sheep in the Highlands that has magnified this danger to the tree's survival, its present weak position is partly due to the law enforced in the last century that outlawed unlicensed distilling of whisky.

For a while secret stills were prolific in the Highlands and the outlaw distillers were aided by the juniper in their secrecy, for burning juniper wood makes the most nearly invisible smoke, easily drifting upward unnoticed by excise inspectors. Juniper was perhaps especially friendly to the distiller for it was about the only tree growing in some of the barren, unfrequented spots chosen for illicit stills. With the great decline in this illicit activity since the first decade of this century the juniper should be on the increase again. But it apprears that the damage done by the whisky outlaws was of relatively little account.

Wherever or whenever juniper numbers in a certain area are low, regeneration is restricted because each individual bears only either male or female flowers, which counteracts, to some extent, its advantage of being both wind-pollinated and insect-pollinated. And the advantage it has in being well-adapted to many soil types is to an extent counteracted by the disadvantage that it has in the two to three years its pollinated female flowers take to develop into seed-bearing fruits. During this time developing fruits must survive the hazards of hungry creatures and extremes of weather.

The present threats are many, yet there are wide areas of land where the juniper is still numerous. Besides, natural evolution has conclusively 'decided' that it is not to be as dominant as it once was. Even in its prime, juniper was not a prolific regenerator, not in relation to trees that colonised soon after it, such as hazel and willow.

The little juniper tree is not likely to disappear from the hills and islands of northern Scotland in the foreseeable future, but its decline over the last century or two would be of great concern to our ancestors if they were to live again, for its properties were once revered and highly valued.

On a practical level, the berries have been valued for the curing of certain ailments, in particular ailments of the stomach. And it was also believed that they could cure epilepsy. Also the fruits of the common juniper, native to most of western Europe, are the basis of gin and in fact the word 'gin' and the word 'juniper' are of the same origin.

Beyond the practical uses, though in some way not unrelated to them, is the role of the juniper in basic occult magic. The berries, or the twigs, or indeed the whole tree, were believed to contain the power to avert the 'evil eye', to be a defence against the harmful spells of one's enemies, be they hostile neighbours or evil spirits. Juniper wood was burnt on the doorstep at *Samhain*, or Hallowe'en, (note the similarity between *Samhain* and *samh*) in order to keep unwanted spirits from the house.

This pagan concept of the tree's power over life's dangers was, like so many ancient traditions, perfectly acceptable to the Christian way of life, as this translation of an old and long-used Gaelic prayer shows,

I will pull the gracious yew (certainly the mountain yew: this prayer comes from the far north west, where the real yew was probably not native at any time)
Through the nine fair ribs of Jesus,
In the name of the Father and the Son and the Spirit of Grace
Against drowning, against danger, against fear.

Warriors and Guardians

Elm

The wych elm, also called Scotch elm, is not uncommon in the Highlands but its principal habitats are in the Border counties and the north of England. Once upon a time there were sizeable forests of wych elm in the south and east of Scotland and in the north east of England but now most are confined to field borders and roadsides. Although certainly native to the Highlands, even quite far north and west, it is in a sense an escapee or refugee from those favoured domains, scattered here and there by the grace of the dominant large hardwoods of the Highlands, oak and ash.

Elms in general are very parochial, having very particular habitats and very particular distinctions in each habitat. There are distinct forms in the different regions of Britain, although strangely enough, there are elms in China of similar form. British elms are quite individual as a group. Within each species of British elm there is a wide and complex variety of localised forms (though distinctions may be very subtle such as a slight variation in the size of leaf) and the Scotch elm is no exception. Thus there are elms in the Highlands with various features distinguishing them from those in, for instance, Peebles-shire. And in fact certain special and valued sub-species developed by man began in the counties on the southern and eastern fringe of the Highlands, such as Perthshire.

In Perthshire and other 'fringe' counties man took unusual forms of the wych elm and crossed them to create new strains for principally ornamental reasons, like the weeping elm and the Camperdown elm, both of which were widely planted in many parts of Britain in the nineteenth century. Presumably the elms on the limits of its most favoured domains spreading into the fairly sudden change to Highland landscape evolved accordingly, to create the distinct forms from which the ornamentals were developed.

The feature general to all wych elms that inspired the botanists and gardeners is its slightly weeping shape, encouraged and exaggerated for the enhancement of parks and gardens. In a natural wych elm in a natural setting, the archetypal shape is tall and straight and regular. In the Highlands specimens are often 'unruly' in appearance. A typical Highland elm has a short trunk, forking into many long limbs reaching in all directions — up, out and down. But 'typical' in the case of the elm can have many versions — as wide and varied as the Highland scenery itself.

Other than its weeping form the wych elm's distinguishing feature is its leaf, which is longer than those of the types native to southern England. Elm leaves are spear-shaped, sometimes wide, sometimes narrow, and they are distinctly toothed and have a rough texture. The small black buds begin to open in late April, just after the flowers appear. The flowers, which are bi-sexual, are in tight clusters of reddish brown petals. From them grow round, flat seed-cases of pale green, containing just one seed. The seeds reach maturity and drop (often carried great distances by the wind) from as early as June till as late as September. And leaves, turning yellow, fall between late September and early November.

The bark of the elm, deeply fissured on the trunks of old specimens, is a pale greyish brown, darkening towards the twigs and becoming shiny and slightly reddish. Its trunk can be more than three feet in diameter, occasionally quite a bit more and in ideal circumstances it exceeds 70 feet in height. Specimens of great girth and great height are usually found only in less wild settings on estate parkland and in sheltered, fertile glens. Those in wilder situations are generally about two to three feet in trunk diameter and about 50 feet in height at most.

Because of the elm's status as a planted or at least encouraged tree in tamer parts it is not easy to define its natural spread. Referring to historical data including soil surveys and mentions in lore and legends, its natural spread in the Highlands is wide. But it is locally thin and scattered with large spaces between habitats. In general it favours places where other large hardwoods are common, usually growing on the borders of the wood or in open spaces within it. It will not grow at a great altitude, significantly less than its common host, the oak, but it can tolerate steep, stony slopes. Because of its virtual dependence on the conditions of established woodland its spread has been affected by the depletion of its companion trees, and its ideal habitats have shrunk accordingly. And yet there has been a degree of compensation, for the separation of woodland into small patches has increased the open fringes that elms favour.

The elm is actually unique in that it does not form into forests like the trees of comparative size, but is scattered singly or in very small groups, being in habit more like rowan or holly than oak or ash. To generalise, the elm is a non-forest tree (particularly in the Highlands), is dependent on the existence of woodland (or at least the recent existence), and requires light and space. This need for light and space was one reason why it never achieved a more dense distribution here, for it was spreading rapidly some seven or eight thousand years ago, colonising regions where improving climate and many centuries of tree-cover (notably birch and hazel) were creating suitable conditions. But it was then thwarted by the even more rapid spread of oak and ash, both of which were especially hardy and versatile. So the elm did have a period when it was widespread and common here, but as such it was temporary and its present distribution, roughly speaking, has been its natural spread for several thousand years.

However, although it is here classed as a non-forest tree there are a few areas where it grows in a certain density. Within the category of forest trees there is variation of degree and the same applies to non-forest trees. The elm only just lies outside the category of forest trees.

Areas where it grows in the greatest density include Arran, south east Argyll, northern Perthshire, southern Banffshire, Easter Ross and eastern and western Inverness-shire. The greatest concentration is in Perthshire and other eastern parts, but there is a surprising density on the island of Skye and the nearby mainland. There is no indication to suggest that these clusters in the rugged west are other than of natural origin.

The Gaelic for elm is *leven* (also *ailm*, but this is not commonly used for placenames). Among the placenames using the word are Loch Leven in Kinross-shire, Loch Leven which separates Argyll and Inverness-shire, and Lephin Carroch in Kintyre. There are a few more but not many — one likely reason is the relative scarcity of elm in the strongholds of Gaelic. Where the elm is most common are in many cases areas where Gaelic placenames have been changed or replaced by the use of other languages, from the Norse and Norman influences of long ago to the more recent spread of English. Accounting for this reason one must bear in mind that the greater days of the elm were thousands of years ago, too long ago to have been an influence on long-standing placenames, and also that some of the elm's present habitats that are within the main Gaelic regions are the result of fairly recent plantings.

Another likely factor to have inhibited the use of the word *leven* is the tree's rather small number of qualities of direct benefit to man. The qualities of most other trees are added to by their use as fuel, but the elm is notoriously poor firewood.

But it does have value for certain specialised products, some traditional and ancient, some of recent or present significance. The timber is strong and slow to rot, withstanding wetness very well and it has had a long tradition in the making of wheels — in some cases all parts were made of elm, in others just the wheel hub, as was common in the chariots used by the North Britons against the Romans. In the fairly recent past long, straight trunks and branches were hollowed for use in plumbing (these were of natural growth or as a result of coppicing). The leaves have been used for making dye and have been greatly valued for feeding livestock, particularly cattle. Trees standing in farmland often have a very straight and even canopy a few feet above the ground, the shoots and buds and leaves of the drooping branches being browsed to the height of cattle with necks full stretched.

A result of, or parallel to, the elm's value to cattle is the old belief that if there is an early fall of its leaves there will be cattle disease in the following year. There are not many other traditional beliefs associated with the elm, nor references to its character in mythology, certainly not widespread and commonly known. Particular individuals or groups have or have had local significance, especially to the south of the Highlands in the elm's most favoured regions.

Nevertheless the same factor applies as to the scant spread of *leven* or *ailm* in placenames, that is the dilution of Gaelic language and tradition in the elm's main Highland habitats. Thus the survival of Highland tree lore in the records and memories of the north and west do not reveal the full status of the elm and though it was never among the most revered of native trees, it almost certainly had a significant quality and character on a wide scale until a few centuries ago.

Perhaps its size and appearance were a part of its particular status, just as they were, and are, relevant to its use as an ornamental tree. Its value, both in natural form and as special hybrid, as an enhancement of landscape has been of special importance over the last couple of centuries, but presumably this is not totally a recent use and it has had older significance. Its aesthetic value, complementing or complemented by its benefits to farming as field boundary and cattle food, indicates a gentle and protective character. And this dual character also signifies its role in nature. It clings to and supports a slope of broken rock, long brown limbs stretching from the base of a wide trunk, the regular pattern of branches and twigs fanning out to a cascade of large bright leaves. Insects and deer feed on the leaves, birds and rodents feed on the plentiful seeds, violets and primroses feed on the leaf litter, and the land is enriched.

Here and there the elm is thriving, aided in part by the offspring of planted specimens, but as a whole it has little security in the Highlands. So many are growing in places used by and easily accessible to man, and are often in his way. It is fairly vigorous as a coppice tree, but is commonly cut back too often for it to regain its reproductive powers, and too few seeds when produced, fall and germinate on land where the seedlings may thrive.

Thankfully Dutch elm disease, which all British elms are prone to, is not prevalent across the Highlands — so far. The disease has devastated the elms of Perthshire and Aberdeenshire, but the beetles which carry the disease have not been able to traverse the empty glens and passes into the West.

Natural changes over centuries and man's former activities affected the elm, but only now does it have to contend with an overall declining fertility in the land. Nevertheless now, and for some time to come at least, wild elms are not hard to find.

Warriors and Guardians

Blackthorn

All native trees have had specific characters or personalities attributed to them. The little blackthorn is one of the best examples illustrating the connection between the supposed character and the facts and features which support it. Like most trees, the character of the blackthorn is variable from story to story or from song to song, but its most usual traits are that of a cunning, rather mischievous personality.

In the ancient symbolic tales it often has the role of the malignant goblin, the evil-doer or to some degree the medium of evil. In some tales about the fairy folk that steal babies, the relieved parents find their stolen infant hidden in the darkness of a blackthorn thicket. In some tales evil spells are transmitted to the intended victims when they prick their hands on the tree's sharp thorns. The original of this tradition is presumably related to the same source as the story Sleeping Beauty. The features of the tree that signify or represent the role as the harbourer or medium of evil are many.

The skin of the blackthorn is dark, darker than all other native trees, and its fruits, the sloes, are also dark and their taste when raw is very sharp. As the song *Killiecrankie* from Perthshire goes, "There are soor slaes (sour sloes) up on Atholl Braes." These features of dark colour, harsh-tasting fruits, and sharp thorns, together with the tree's twisted shape, combine to create the blackthorn's negative, inhospitable image.

Yet each, in one way or another, is a part of the tree's beneficial qualities — aesthetic, ecological and practical — and these were not totally excluded from the old stories and songs. There is no clear barrier between the negative and the positive characteristics, and indeed what may seem a bad trait could be interpreted otherwise. For example, the density and sharpness of a blackthorn thicket may make it seem inhospitable yet these features could be interpreted as protective, as many farmers of many ages have recognised.

Being fast to grow, hardy, dense and thorny, black-thorns are the ideal protection for crops and livestock. In the areas where they grow best they have been long valued for hedging, either mixed with other trees, such as hawthorn, planted against stone dykes, or used alone.

Another use of blackthorn which can have a positive

or negative image according to interpretation is the making of clubs — the Irish *sheleilaigh* of tradition. In such a form the wood is a frightening weapon, yet this, like other features, could be said to be a protective trait.

Blackthorn is also commonly used in the making of walking sticks, in recognition of which the dance tune *Blackthorn Stick* was composed. Craftsmen who have (and to some extent still do so) fashioned blackthorn walking sticks have always valued blackthorn trunks or branches that have been shaped by the spiralling growth of honeysuckle or other climbers. The effect of the climbing plants on the tree is quite spectacular, and the stick cut from such a tree is the traditional crooked stick of the kilted Highlander, still a popular image.

The duality of the blackthorn's personality is also characterised by the tree's fruits, the hard, dark sloes. The flavour that underlies the harsh taste of the raw, unsweetened sloe has been recognised and appreciated over a wide area and for a long, long time. The juice added to gin makes the celebrated sloe gin, but the fruit can itself be the foundation of an alcoholic beverage, or can be boiled with apples to make sloe jelly.

These are just some of the things that can be produced by cooking or processing the fruit of the blackthorn, yet over a longer time, with knowledge, skill and patience, the blackthorn has been transformed to become the chief strain of most of our plum trees. Encouraged, nurtured and selected the blackthorn tree gave us first the damson, then, crossed with the cherry plum of western Asia, the large sweet plums of our modern orchards and gardens. All these benefits of the little blackthorn tree would not convince a person of strongly superstitious beliefs that it was not particularly malignant, but that person might at least concede to the sentiments of this old saying translated from the Gaelic, "Better the bramble than the blackthorn, but better the blackthorn than the devil."

The dark, spiky, twisting form of the blackthorn tree is contrasted by the white flush of its blossom in April, then by the bright green of its leaves in May, and later by the yellow of its leaves, which may stay upon the branches until the beginning of December.

The tree, and all its features, are not particularly vulnerable to severe weather, though prevailing conditions affect the height and shape of individuals. On the hillocks of the west coast and the islands the winds will make sure that most specimens will not exceed about five or six feet in height, while those with reasonable shelter will reach about 12 feet. But even with the best conditions there will be no certainty of height and form. One may be tall and narrow while a neighbour of the same age will be low and spreading. Similarly, there is no certainty that particular conditions of climate and ground will produce a tree rich in fruit. One tree has almost no fruit, another nearby is laden, and this situation is liable to persist from year to year.

Such subtleties and peculiarities are not easily defined, but were at least recognised by the horticulturalists in their selective search for the specimens that were the parents of the original damson trees and plum trees. Certain birds, in fact many kinds, get to know the best trees and nest in, under or near them. Few birds will actually eat large quantities of sloes but some, in particular finches, will eat a lot if they sense the approach of a hard winter. Birds help the tree's seed dispersal, as do some small rodents, and it also increases itself by suckers from the roots.

Unfortunately its low and twisted form means that to modern eyes it is no more than an unwanted shrub, and its numbers are becoming too few in many parts of the Highlands. It is not likely to decline much further in the foreseeable future, but it is likely to disappear from some of its wilder habitats if modern systems of land-use are maintained. Isolated patches of blackthorn exist in most regions and in islands of the west, and the tree is not rare inland and in the north east.

Its favourite companion tree seems to be hazel, and blackthorns will often be found on the eaves of a hazel copse or wood.

The Gaelic name *drain* or *draoighean* is a fairly common component in placenames and these show the natural distribution of blackthorn. Examples are Glendrain in Ardnamurchan, Port na Droighearn on Islay, and Ardindrean in Wester Ross. But another Gaelic name for the tree is *sluach*, presumably related to the word 'sloe', although the most usual Gaelic word for the fruit of the tree is *airneag*.

Warriors and Guardians

Hawthorn

The hawthorn tree is a cousin of the blackthorn, but there are many trees in the British Isles of the same rose family. Because of this family connection there are similarities in laws of growth, and in benefits, but the differences are many. The hawthorn, though of greater size — and partly because of greater size — is not so well adapted as the blackthorn to extreme conditions. But it is still a hardy tree and can be found growing wild in some of Scotland's least fertile regions.

Because it has been extensively planted for hedging,

more than any other tree of the Highlands, it is not easy to establish the parts where it is truly native. But it may be presumed that virtually all Highland counties support hawthorns of wild origin, including most of the sizeable Hebridean islands. Among the areas where they are particularly common are Mid-Argyll, Kintyre, Dunbartonshire, Perthshire, Moray and Easter Ross, with some significant clusters in Skye and Lochaber. In these areas, and in other parts of the southern Highlands, hedges of hawthorn are quite common, or at least the remains of them — often no more than a very incomplete line of old specimens, sometimes at intervals along an unmaintained stone dyke between fields or a field and a road.

Individual hawthorns that have been regularly lopped and layered will not, if left untended, ever reach the height of a wild specimen which in certain conditions may reach 30 feet. One of this height is most commonly seen on the edge of woodland or in an enclosed gully where soil is rich, wind is gentle and light is moderate. Such a specimen is likely to have fewer branches and less foliage than those that grow in different conditions and reach 20 feet or less. Out in the meadows, with damp ground, deep soil and a lot of light the hawthorn tends to be low but with a multitude of spreading branches, the lowest being very close to or even touching the ground. On broken slopes of granite and limestone, exposed to winds, mature trees may be only 6 feet high, but still have many branches and dense foliage, appearing as a ball of green on the pale grey slope.

With a reasonable balance of all conditions and a strong, healthy parentage, a hawthorn can live for 300 years — exceptional for a tree of its size. Its longevity is of course a significant part of its hedging value and this has always been the tree's greatest practical benefit to us and an added security to its own continuity. But its timber has also been valued and in the past that has been to its benefit and not a threat.

The timber has been used for small, decorative carvings and for bowls and other small household items and its resiliant toughness makes it ideal for tool handles. The wood is quite good as a fuel but there has not been extensive felling for this purpose, which is fortunate for the tree does not coppice well and may even die when felled.

When there has been a long, cold winter, when new growth is slow to come to the land, the hawthorn still brings forth its bright leaves in early April and in the past hungry people were glad to pick and eat them. The fruits, the little red haws, are not very palatable to humans straight from the tree but may be made into, or added to, a jelly or a drink. Quite a few birds eat haws, but only sparingly when they are first ripe, for they keep well on the tree for a long time and can be invaluable if midwinter is very harsh. The haws are especially valued by blackbirds and thrushes.

In myth and legend the cuckoo has a special affinity with the hawthorn tree. Both have a special role in the tales that symbolise the birth of summer, the final freedom from winter.

In the tale of Thomas the Rhymer, the poet and seer of the thirteenth century, Thomas was in the hills of southern Scotland when he met an Elven Queen by a hawthorn tree from which a cuckoo was calling. The tree's role in tradition and ancient ritual has a definite female aspect. The Fairy Queen that leads Thomas into her own world for seven years of earthly time is a version, or representative, of the Goddess that presided over moonlit rituals in groves of hawthorn long, long ago. Circles of hawthorn trees formed sacred enclosures for private ritual worship of the Lady that rode on the moon, whose light in early summer reflected on the clusters of white flowers adorning the 'whitethorn' trees. The belief that this tree has a strong affinity with things beyond the obvious world has persisted for thousands of years, and even today there are Highland people who will not have hawthorn blossom brought into the home, it being, like some other white flowers, a symbol of things outside human life, a sacred and untouchable thing of the wild.

The month of flowering is the month of May (usually late May), traditionally the time when domestic life should not be allowed to encroach upon our wilder instincts, when plants of the wild should not be exploited or harmed, especially the hawthorn — the 'May Tree'. Just how widespread and long-lived the practice of worship in hawthorn groves in the Highlands may have been is impossible to judge, but perhaps some of the places bearing its Gaelic name *sgitheach*, testify to local observance at some time.

There also appears to have been some special link between the tree and hereditary chiefs. On one West Highland estate there is a cluster of hawthorn trees which, it is said, are connected with a curse or prediction made by an old spey-wife. Should the trees be felled, the laird's line will come to an end. The trees are now close to a natural death and the laird's family are thriving — and this happens to be a locally popular laird! At another location in the North East Highlands a very famous castle was built over a hawthorn tree and some centuries later the tree was still alive in the building's cellar.

Examples of placenames referring to the hawthorn tree include Loch Sgitheeach on Jura, Achadh na Sgitheach in Cowal, Abhain Sgitheach in Easter Ross and Loch Skiach in Perthshire. The Gaelic name for the tree's fruits is *sgichean* — an area of Mull bears this name. In older Gaelic the hawthorn has also been *uath*, but I know of no placenames using this word.

In some of the areas where hawthorn has been quite common it will not now be seen but it is fairly secure in the Highlands as a whole. With just a little more regard given to it when men are clearing ground it will flourish again.

Willow

The beautiful weeping willow was brought in relatively recent times from China and is not native to the Highlands. But there are many forms of willow, too many in fact for there to be an agreed number. The willow has had plenty of time to diversify itself for it colonised rapidly on the heels of the last Ice Age and has been widespread and numerous for 12,000 years.

The different forms of willow can be put into three convenient groups but each group is diverse and lines between can be blurred. The origins of the many specific forms are uncertain for there are types within each group that can cross with another within that group, and some that cross with others outside the group. All of which is further complicated by man's long and frequent practice of encouraging hybrids so to extend the values of willow, most especially its value in wicker-work. Thus there are hybrids that may or may not have formed naturally, just as there are types which may or may not be true hybrids.

The features of regeneration common to all willows are that male and female catkins are borne on separate specimens, pollen is transferred by insects and their tiny seeds have fine hairs which allow them to be carried far by the wind. Other common features are that all types coppice vigorously and all can be grown from cuttings.

The most prolific group is that of the sallows, then the osiers, then a less specific, less defined group made up of crack-willow, white-willow and bay-willow. The white-willow, which can cross with crack-willow, is probably not native to the Highlands, but the other two of the group are, if only just. Most recognised types of osier are native to the Highlands, and most of the numerous types of sallow.

Crack and bay-willow very occasionally crossbreed but both are rare in the Highlands, especially the former. Crack-willow can be up to 60 feet high and they have a wide spreading crown on a wide, usually short trunk. Bay-willows reach about 40 feet, often with a multi-stemmed trunk and with suckers from the long roots. The catkins of each are similar — pale green female catkins and yellow male, though the male are a particularly bright yellow on the bay. Those of crack appear in late April or early May, and those of bay almost a month later. The leaves of both are finely toothed: those of crack are long and narrow and pale green; those of bay are wider and a dark glossy green. They both grow only on ground that is constantly wet and they require good light and a mild climate to reach a good size. The types of loam soil of the parts to the south where they flourish best are rare in the Highlands but they manage well enough by some rivers of the southern foothills, particularly in Dunbartonshire, Perthshire and Stirlingshire. And there are parts of the west coast where bay-willow is quite numerous, notably Lorn in Argyll and the south-western coasts of Sutherland.

Osiers are the most difficult to individually identify and categorise. Hybridisation is fairly common in the wild, and because the osiers are the best for the once important skill of basketry, many special hybrids have been created by man. Three forms can be positively established as pure — the common osier, the almond-leafed willow and the purple osier. All grow in a towering shape with many long straight stems and all have narrow leaves. Pure almond willows and purple osiers are very rare in the wild but are probably native to most Highland counties.

Common osiers are relatively numerous, especially in the West Highlands. Probably most almond and purple and about half of common osier now seen here would have been planted, or at least be of planted parentage. This is evident by their frequent proximity to old cottages and empty and otherwise treeless townships in the Outer Isles. Of the few areas where osiers have a strong claim to natural, local origin many if not most are in Argyll where there are low coastal flats with a warm, wet climate, conditions similar to their greatest domains in southwest England.

Sallows are extremely hard to positively identify and, although this is in other ways the most specific, defined group, experts rarely agree on the number of pure sallow types. The largest can be 50 feet high while some types do not exceed a few inches. These tiny forms, the dwarf willows and Arctic willows are excluded here and (thankfully !) they do not cross with the sallows of tree size.

The next type up in size could also be considered too small to be called a tree. The round-eared sallow is spreading, dense and often a perfect dome shape, growing to about 15 feet in height, often much less in exposed areas or places of thin soil. The leaves, from which it takes its name, are small, almost oval and usually of rough texture. Colour of leaves, like shape and texture, is variable but generally a greyish green. The twigs are a dull grey but often tinged with dark red. The little catkins of the male tree are white and yellow, those of the female are green and remain on the tree well into July. This type, or a sub-species of it, is sometimes called woolly or downy willow. Whether those with 'hairy' leaves are distinct from smoother-leafed round-eared willows is debatable, though in general the 'hairier' forms are most common in the north and north west, or in the higher harsher habitats of all parts.

Slightly taller, though less spreading and bushy, is the grey willow or common sallow. Trunk and twigs are pale grey and it grows to about 25 feet in height. Leaves are more regularly oval than those of lesser sallows and are pale green, particularly on the underside. Their catkins are similar to those of the round-eared willow. But shape, size and colouring of leaves are very variable and since it crosses readily with all other sallows of tree size, pure forms are difficult to detect among a great range of hybrids.

The largest sallow is the great sallow, of which there may be more than one distinct form, but whose principal distinction is its size. Great sallows of full size, up to 60 feet and occasionally more, are not very common and it is possible that some of the many smaller great sallow-type specimens are in fact mature members of a sub-species.

The great sallow is the willow commonly called pussy willow, a name descriptive of its furry catkins. It is also called goat willow for its leaves are favoured by goats and other browsing animals. The leaves make this tree easily distinguishable from other willows, although it does occasionally cross with common osier. Leaves of pure great sallow are large and wide and actually resemble the leaves of the apple tree more than the small or spear-shaped leaves of other willows. They are fairly smooth above and a light but bright green. Below they are downy and almost white. In autumn they are an attractive lemon-yellow and may remain in some density on the tree until late November. They are irregularly toothed on the edge, often wavy. The catkins are large and are more rounded than the otherwise similar catkins of the common osier. They appear slightly earlier than the leaves, in late March or early April. The male catkins quickly turn from silver to yellow-gold and the female catkins become large and solid and pale green in colour. During May the female catkins open up and, like those of the common osier, they become like tufts of wool. The bark is usually pale grey but occasionally it is a darker grey. Though the bark is generally smooth it sometimes cracks a bit on particularly old specimens. The winter buds and twigs feature an attractive display of colour, the buds varying from pale green to orange and the twigs from dark green to deep red. The twig pattern of the great sallow also distinguishes it from other sallows for the twigs are particularly thick, straight and regular. Those of other sallows are relatively brittle and they grow in all directions, creating a dense mesh of short twigs.

Most forms of sallow are widespread in the Highlands. The lesser types, especially the round-eared or woolly willows, are often referred to as scrub willow, an accurate if not very flattering term for these types are usually low and spreading. Scrub willow is found in all the Highland counties, including most of the Hebridean and Northern islands. Its habitats are very varied in soil type, climate and altitude, and it is absent only from exceptionally well drained slopes in the eastern Highlands where rainfall is relatively low. It is commonly a tree of riverside and marshland but can be found on high ridges and moors close to meagre springs and burns. On wooded hills solitary specimens of scrub willow grow among the birches, being most obvious in early winter when it still has many leaves that cast a spray of green in an almost bare forest.

In late winter many of the numerous little willows in the hills and upland birch forests are seen to be largely stripped of bark, having provided sustenance for foraging deer.

Forms of scrub willow sometimes cross with grey willow and between the pure forms of each is an array of hybrids. The grey willow, like scrub willow, enjoys a range of habitats although they do not tolerate such altitudes. Therefore hybrids are confined to areas suited to both, such as coastal heaths and bogs in the south west. In its pure form grey willow is fairly widespread but rare in the north and north east. It is abundant in the long glens of the mid-southern Highlands such as Glenaray and Strathyre.

The distribution of the great sallow is much the same as that of the grey willow. In most localities it is more thinly distributed than the grey, except for parts of the south west. It is particularly common on the shores of some of Argyll's more sheltered sea lochs, for instance Loch Fyne and Loch Feochan. If one is looking for crack willows one should look in more or less the same areas favoured by the great sallow although any found north of Argyll and Perthshire are almost certainly not of natural origin. Yet it is possible that it is native on Speyside.

Taking into account size, distribution and natural benefits, it is probable that placenames with the Gaelic word for willow, which is *shelloch*, refer almost exclusively to the great sallow and to the common osier. Such placenames, some of which use the older form of the Gaelic such as *suil*, are very common throughout the Highlands. Among them are Ardshealach and Glensuileag in Inverness-shire, Corrieshalloch (the National Nature Reserve in Speyside) and Auchnashelloch in Argyll. Historically such placenames bear witness both to the presence of willows as a natural feature and to local basket and related industries.

Yet they also reflect an ancient and deep reverence for the species. While some of the customs and legends associated with willow are of an esoteric nature, in general they reflect or complement its down-to-earth qualities very closely and perhaps symbolise the connection between usage and superstition more clearly than those of any other tree. The vitality of the tree's coppice and pollard growth is exceptional, often resulting in stems several feet high in just one year. This fact, together with the strength and pliancy of the stems as well as the ease with which a new tree can be made by simply pushing a stem or twig into the earth, has been of great value to the prosperity and stability of rural life.

For thousands of years willow wands have served the wicker industry in all its diversity — lobster pots, bee-hives, chairs and a virtually infinite variety of baskets for seed, for harvest, for wood and for peat. Such valued products could in themselves have given the tree an important place in myth and magic, but there have been other important factors. For a long, long time, it was believed that parts of willow, especially flowering twigs, emanated or promoted health and they were cut and gathered to be brought into the home. Of similar origin was the use of willow in the church's celebration of Palm Sunday when it took the place of palm, which was of course largely unavailable in this country. This practice was widespread in Britain and Ireland and even now is not entirely vanished.

The customs in recognition of the tree's health-giving properties are supported by its real and provable features. For instance, the 'wool' of the matured catkins was once used to make a lint for protecting and healing damaged skin. This is a practical, understandable use of catkins but in the past such use was extended quite naturally into what might be called sympathetic magic in order to transmit the qualities of the tree. This aspect is revealed in this old Highland poem revering the lady saint, Bride:

Pluck will I myself the catkin wool,
The lint the lovely Bride culled through her palm,
For success, for cattle, for increase,

For pairing, for uddering, for milking,
For female calves white-bellied
As was spoken in the prophecy.

But perhaps the property of the willow that most clearly supports the superstitious traditions, and which is scientifically verifiable, lies in one of its chemical components — the drug salacin, from which the original aspirin was made.

There were other traditions that were not connected with the willow's health-giving properties, at least not directly. Most people have read or heard tales of wizards and their magical willow wands. Such images almost certainly stem from the use of willow by Druids who employed it in matters of divination and justice. They probably also used willow medicinally as a drug, as a lint or in acts of sympathetic magic.

The willow's connection with justice had a later representation when a peeled wand was the rod of justice held by the Lords of the Isles. The wand was also held by the Lords when they were initiated, a practice which was continued by most major clan chiefs. A number of the tree's features and qualities could have given rise to this tradition — its appearance, its vitality, its health-renewing properties, its very important role as host to an assortment of plants and creatures, all of which could suitably symbolise the fundamental responsibilities of a lord or chief. Yet the specific feature of the peeled willow wand itself that surely symbolised the initiate's representation of truth and justice is its whiteness.

Like many other trees the traditions associated with the willow represent qualities both of a symbolic nature, such as strength and harmony, and of everyday use.

There were rituals and customs that evoked the inner characteristics of the tree, but many others that were in imitation or recognition of its practical, usable qualities. Most of these were basically local and correspond not only to local requirements but also to the particular forms of willow. There were for instance, customs in certain areas that corresponded to the making of small items from the timber of the great sallow by gypsies and travellers, notably the traditional clothes peg. The timber is excellent for turning and was used for making wheel spokes for Celtic chariots. Similarly, in certain areas there were traditions associated with the growing, selection, cutting, preparing and use of osiers — anything from locally used nicknames to taboos restricting the cutting of osiers at certain times such as the wane of the moon. Some of these traditions are still observed in parts of Britain like Somerset where osier production for basket making is still important.

To wildlife organisations, individual enthusiasts and conservationists willows have a special importance as hosts to a great variety of plants and creatures. There are the insects, notably bees and hoverflies that transfer the pollen; the furry caterpillars, often hundreds to a tree, that feed on the leaves; the fish and other creatures of rivers, pools and lochs that feed and breed under the willows; the birds, such as warblers, that nest in the density of willow scrub.

Of all the willows, and indeed of all trees, probably the most hospitable of hosts is the crack willow. The crack willow, so named because of its relatively brittle twigs, has commonly been treated as a pollard — cut at the top of the trunk — and in this way its benefit to wildlife has been increased. In the sheltered hollows of the mature pollard, in between the numerous straight growth stems, many forms of life take up residence, from mosses and ferns to mushrooms and even foxgloves, from beetles to birds and even snakes.

Willows in general are endangered in the Highlands, not just the naturally rare crack willow and bay willow, but also the osiers and great sallows. Even though the lopping and felling rarely harm the resilient willow, and can even increase their years, continued action of this kind on a more or less regular basis greatly affects chances of reproduction. In many areas willows are being killed outright by changes in land-use and in fact suitable habitats for recolonisation are becoming ever fewer.

The security and diversity of our wildlife are being badly affected by the depletion of the willow. Be they for baskets, for their ecological qualities or for their beauty, the willows should have a future allowed them.

Holly

The evergreen holly, our only broad-leaf evergreen, hangs on to survival resolutely yet with sparing energy. Its spiked leaves deter the damaging grazers and browsers yet the young seedlings are susceptible to the excesses of frost, rain or drought they may have to endure. And the young leaves are soft and eaten by various creatures, from snails to deer.

Isolated hollies growing on rocky slopes or under large trees thrive there alone for a long, long time, a century and a half or more, yet the very nature of such habitats can restrict the advance of their offspring. The favourite habitat of holly is oak forest, where it enjoys the soil rich in leaf-mould and where it is compatible with the companion plants and creatures of oak. Yet in the shade of the large trees new hollies are deprived of required light and few will reach maturity.

Another way in which the tree's governing laws restrict its advance is its system of sexual reproduction. One specimen is either male or female and as most grow in isolation the little white flowers of the female tree may not receive pollen from a male tree and thus be barren of seed-bearing fruits. Most females, in most seasons however, do receive pollen, thanks to butterflies and other flies travelling the distance between female and male tree. This is a precarious method of reproduction yet very occasionally one may find a holly bearing both male and female flowers. It is as if the holly has a conscious desire to remain sparsely distributed, changing its own laws when or where that distribution is too sparse, creating an individual that ensures the local survival of the species by producing both genders.

In its rarity, and its almost secretive nature, lies the holly's special character. Alone on a face of broken rock or deep in a forest of oak the holly is a sudden and welcome sight, especially in winter with dark, glossy green leaves that never fail and distinctive crimson berries. New foliage in May and June replaces sporadic loss of leaves in the winter. The berries remain all winter and birds will generally eat them only when the season is unusually severe. Because of its appearance at this time, holly has long been harvested as a decoration for the home, bringing colour and life to brighten winter days, reminding us that life goes on. In the same way it is the ideal decoration for the festivities of Christmas, representing the eternal aspects of life, and symbolising the thorny crown of Christ in its spiky leaves and the blood of Christ in its crimson berries. It is quite common to see a holly tree in small churchyards, instead of and sometimes as well as the more usual yew tree.

In more ancient lore, lore that has survived within Gaelic poetry and proverbs, the character of the holly is seen as protective, like other evergreens having the power to ward off evil spells. The spikes of its leaves probably have something to do with this. One invocation calling for protection begins, "To thorny trees and hollies . . . "

However, another old Gaelic charm of protection uses the holly to represent the evil which its reciting is supposed to ward off, "The wicked who would do me harm . . . Be it fiercer, sharper, harsher, more malignant than the hard, wounding holly."

Whichever personality was accorded to the holly, protective or malignant, it has certainly been incorporated into acts of sympathetic magic. Another translation of a Gaelic saying reveals this feature, though its meaning is not absolutely clear, ". . . when the hag (here meaning either 'wise-woman' or 'priestess') fails to keep the grass under, she throws the mallet at the root of the holly tree."

There have been taboos against felling, or even lopping, holly trees. Yet restricted cutting, or using the dead or dying specimens, has provided the people of the Highlands with useful and attractive timber. Statuettes and wood for inlayed work have been shaped from the hard, white timber, and its strength has made it useful for the handles of weapons and tools.

But of course, living trees are also of great benefit to us for they can make solid, long-living, impregnable hedges.

Hedges of holly may be seen over much of the Highlands but are less common or non-existent where other good hedge trees are more abundant or where stone is the most practical material for enclosure, or of course where the holly is not found in the wild.

Because it is relatively common and because of specific systems of agriculture, it has been used for hedging most widely in the southern and south-eastern Highlands, particularly where the mountainous terrain slopes to the gentler farm-lands of Dunbartonshire, Perthshire, Stirlingshire and Angus. Otherwise, in its wild state, it is most common in the coastal regions of Argyll, western Inverness-shire, and Wester Ross, growing most abundantly in parts where oak is common, such as Cowal, Knapdale, Loch Awe, Sunart, Moidart and Ardgower. Holly is fairly common in parts of Sutherland and on some of the islands, including Mull and Colonsay. It is the cap badge of the Mull McLeans and the Knapdale Macmillans. Its Gaelic name *chuilinn* is seen in placenames throughout these regions — Cruach-doire-cuilean on Mull, Camus a Chuilinn in Ardgower, Meall a Chuillin in Sunart, Stron Chuilinn in Cowal, and Gualachulain in Glen Etive.

Shape and size of holly trees is very variable. Their tendency is to grow to a pointed crown, appearing rather like most firs and spruces, but conditions of ground and climate, being so variable in the Highlands, cause a wide variety of shapes.

With 'perfect' conditions the pale grey trunk will be smooth and regular, tapering to a height of 40 feet with an abundance of regular narrow branches, all dense with foliage. In less than perfect circumstances the trunk may divide not far from the ground, and may be twisted and narrow, with branches of irregular form and with sparse foliage. In dense woodland they grow in an unruly form, with long slender branches sweeping the ground, which sometimes root themselves in the leaf-mould to form 'new' trees. Once a holly is established, even at only three or four years old, there is very little that will halt its growth. Younger than this it is vulnerable to extreme frost and the soft young leaves are likely to be nibbled by sheep, cattle, deer and even rabbits.

There are few records or references to show us the extent of the holly in the past, as compared to the present distribution. Yet this lack itself suggests that it has never been significantly more common than it is now. However, the present ratio of young to old is not as it should be. There are mature hollies in oak forest where excessive grazing is recent and these are not being replaced by healthy 'youngsters'. There are mature hollies growing in open, mostly tree-less glens, survivors from the time when these glens were wooded — before the wild woods were cut down 'wholesale' for feeding hungry furnaces.

In places, for example Nature Reserves, roadsides and lochsides, there are still young hollies to be seen, and in comparison to some other non-forest trees, the species is not in great danger of Highland extinction. But without revised policies for land use whole regions that have supported the holly for thousands of years will soon be without this special tree sustaining itself in the wild.

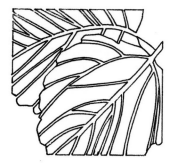

Alder

The dark alder is a fast growing, hardy tree, widespread and numerous in the Highlands. There are a great many varieties spread across Europe. Just how many forms are native here is very difficult to ascertain, but such variation as there might be is slight and all can be safely said to belong to the group called *alder glutinosa.*

The alder habitat greatly affects the size and shape of the tree (at least as much as its relative the birch even though its range of habitats is not so great). Where a particular form is created is entirely due to prevailing conditions. Whether a particular form is a distinct sub-species special to the prevailing conditions is a complicated and perhaps indefinable subject. In general, it is safe to say that one specimen's size and shape is the result of its habitat and the events in the history of its growth. One such event that is significant is the lopping or felling of the tree, creating a vigorous coppice form of growth.

Coppiced alders are in fact more common than uncoppiced and one can become so used to the resulting shape that one can be very surprised by the appearance of an alder that has reached maturity untouched by saw or axe. Coppiced alders are neat and regular, a dense collection of straight and tall stems with an even profusion of branches and twigs reaching out and up towards a conical crown. The pointed crown is the tendency of untouched alders as well, but conditions usually give the matured tree a more open, irregular crown.

Alder wood's deep colour and attractive grain gave it the name, Scotch Mahogany.

On the whole, natural growth that is most similar to the typical coppice specimen is most commonly seen where conditions are open, well-drained and/or at a certain altitude. On open heath, for instance, poor soil and a lot of wind cause it to grow small and bushy. Similarly the wind and drainage of a wide river's banks where it flows through low meadows close to the sea, causes it to be pointed and not too tall, if perhaps less bushy with one or two trunks. At a certain altitude all these conditions may be present and again the alder will be pointed, narrow of trunk or trunks and not very tall.

The alder does not grow at anything like the altitude known to its cousin the birch. It is only in the river gullies that run down the Highland hills that it can be found much above sea-level, for here it has the moisture it requires. In the damp and shadowy gullies, often among tall birches and ash trees, it grows tall and lean — few of branch and tangle-crowned, thriving on the local ecological system yet also contributing greatly to it.

But it is on lower ground that the largest alders are seen — where rivers and burns spread into pools; in mires among hillocks and knolls or just where rain water lies long. Here they may reach 70 feet in height with a trunk of three feet in diameter or more. One with such a girth of trunk narrows quickly, making it sort of bulbous at the bottom, narrowing to perhaps half that width within a few feet, then tapering only gradually towards the high, twisty branches of the irregular crown. From the bulbous base, and from the roots, there are often many narrow shoots rising, but above them the trunk may be branchless for 20 feet or more. If the typical or average alder is that as seen fringing a wide river — lean, straight, bushy and pointed — then the alder is in its fullest flourishing and in its absolute element when it grows in these sheltered mires.

This is the place called alder swamp, where the bushy trunks 'sit' in the still water — a dense ground cover, then a more open space, then a dark closed canopy — a still, damp, dim forest, unruly yet vibrant and lush. A similar habitat is formed in miniature on flat bog-land, but in either location there is this special private yet fertile habitat. Seeds of alder colonise pockets of good soil and water on flat bogs or among rocky knolls beneath high hills and they add their special qualities to these places. The isolation, the closedness, and the swampiness of these places feature deeply in the lore and mythology of the Highlands.

Secrecy, refuge and privacy are the aspects of the alder's role in mythological tradition. In the alder woods of Argyll, Diarmid and Grainne, the eloping lovers, hid from Finn MacCuil and his warriors, and here also Deidre hid herself when the soldiers of the rejected King Conchobar followed her from Ireland. And ever since the far-off era of these myths or events, runaways, outlaws, outcasts and rebels have found safe refuge in the dimness of alder forests. The refuge can be as much for bad as for good, and in some tales of the Highlands or other parts of Britain, and Ireland, the 'closedness' of the forest has a slightly sinister character.

Marion Campbell, the Argyll author and historian, suggested to me that a certain fear regarding alders related to the fact that the tree's timber turns red when cut, like blood. This feature and the density of the forest combine with the darkness of the tree's limbs to create this more sinister aspect of its character, yet in a positively down-to-earth, tangible sense it really is a welcoming refuge for it adds so much to its location.

One special way in which it enhances the fertility of its environment is the action of its roots in taking nitrogen from the air and adapting it to the soil and the needs of the plants that grow there, including itself. In this way and many others the environs of an alder swamp or copse or forest is the ideal habitat for many plants and creatures, some of them otherwise not very common. Wood-violets, primroses, garlic, mint and clover carpet the damp ground, ivy and honeysuckle festoon the tall trees, royal ferns and great sprays of sedge thrive in the gaps between, and where the alders are well spaced there are rows and clusters of tall yellow iris. The trees are also shelter and sustenance to the alder moth caterpillar, to finches and wildfowl that eat the seeds of the tree, to water-shrews, otters and badgers, to frogs and fish.

Some of these life-forms are of course specific to the vicinity of burns and rivers. The burrows and holts of shrews and of otters can be found among the roots of old riverside alders, their homes or nests protected by the alders and their food ready to hand. Fish often congregate in the shade of alders in early spring, part of the food chain from alder to its companion flowers to insects to fish to otters and so on. It is no accident that anglers watch for the first opening of the alder's leaf buds.

Moving water also adds another dimension to the alder's dispersal for the seeds that fall on the water are adapted to float and may germinate when they lodge on a bank. The female catkins that carry the seeds sometimes fall or are blown down, before all the seeds have dropped, but they are rounded and woody and also adapted to float, so carrying seeds downstream. They actually closely resemble small cones, and like those of conifer trees, they do not shed seed until well into winter, even late winter. In the early stage they are very small and a bright pink, and it is at this time they are fertilised by pollen from the opening male catkins usually from late February to mid-March. The male catkins are long and a dark maroon, becoming green as they open. The twigs are a sort of orange/maroon, and the leaf buds are protected from cold by a purple film. The almost round and finely toothed leaves appear in late April or early May, and they have a stickiness which provides a certain protection against flies and caterpillars. In sheltered positions the dark green leaves remain on the tree well into November.

The leaves, and also the bark, have been widely used for making dye. The timber of the alder is now hardly used but has had a number of special uses in the past. Because of its resistance to water it was valued for making walkways, water-wheels, piers, bridges and lock-gates, and even clogs. Its quality charcoal was used for smelting and also as a base for making gunpowder. It has also been valued by furniture makers for its deep colour and attractive grain, qualities which gave it the name 'Scotch Mahogany'.

The alder is widespread and common throughout Britain and Ireland but it has retained a particular density over a longer time here in the Scottish Highlands. Although significantly depleted in recent times with changes in land use it has not been so radically affected as it has in, for instance, the east of England, where large areas of its natural habitat have been lost due to great works of drainage. The Highland terrain and climate not only encourage the growth of alders but actually protect them — deep, fertile glens and gullies, gathering the rains from steep mountains, and places where people and even sheep rarely venture. And yet, paradoxically, the largest area of alder in the Highlands, which is in fact the largest in all Britain, owes not a little to fairly recent efforts by man to increase land productivity. This is the Mound alder forest in Sutherland where the building of a causeway created an unnaturally large area of wetland where the alders are thriving in great density.

But all along the long narrow glens of Sutherland and Caithness the alder has thrived for thousands of years, since their colonisation some eight to nine thousand years ago on the heels of the Ice Age, and all over the Highlands there are clusters, belts and forests of alder of ancient origin. It is one of the few trees to grow naturally and continuously in the Outer Hebrides, though it is not easily found there. It is particularly common in Lochaber, Moidart, Knapdale and Cowal, and in parts of Perthshire, Angus and Morayshire.

In Gaelic it is called *fearn*. It has given its name to Fearn in Easter Ross, Ardfern and Alltfearna in Argyll, Glen Fearnach in Perthshire, and to a great many other places.

The refuges of alder in the Highlands are many, and in a number of them the alders are large and close, and indeed there are many areas where man has allowed new forests to begin. But many of these refuges are set to disappear in the near future. In such places they are now patches of scrub, regularly cut back, and although cutting increases their life-span it can obliterate their capability to reproduce, even if there are several years between each cut. Nevertheless, if one is prepared to go off the beaten track (and get wet feet!) one can still enter the dim, secret, verdant timelessness of ancient alder forest.

Hazel

The hazel is one of the most common trees of the Highlands. It has grown here for about 10,000 years, being hardy to the semi-tundra conditions that followed the Ice Age. In the present day its greatest domains in the British Isles are here. It grows as a forest tree in its own right and also as a common companion to other forest trees.

In Gaelic it is called *coll* and *calltuinn* and has given its name to a number of places, particularly in the west. Among them are the island of Coll, Cnoc a'Challtuinn on Mull, Barr Calltuinn in Appin and Barcaldine (*barr calltuinn*).

These are all in Argyll. Relevant placenames are not common elsewhere and indeed no other county in the Highlands, nor anywhere in Britain, has such a prolific hazel population.

Soil tests have shown that it was once extremely prolific almost everywhere, even in the Orkneys and the Shetlands, but climatic changes caused it to dwindle, aided a bit by the spread of people. For the last few thousand years it has been rare in the far north and north-west, yet it is still found in parts of otherwise virtually tree-less areas such as the Outer Isles. Isolated specimens and small copses are dotted here and there about the Central and Eastern Highlands, but it is most numerous in the mid-west, the south-west and the south, on a sort of curve from Wester Ross through western Inverness-shire, Argyll and Dunbartonshire (where it is the clan badge of the Colquhouns) to western Perthshire.

Being a tree that is hardy, resilient and versatile it seems surprising that it is not so common outside this curve. The hazel does not have the sort of spread of the birch, with which it has certain significant similarities – size, adaptability to different soils and to different degrees of wetness, and the time-span of its existence. Both the birch and the hazel were prolific in virtually all parts of the Highlands and Islands some eight to ten thousand years ago.

Apparently the hazel has a tendency to the wetter, warmer regions. This is a bit of a paradox, considering its rapid colonisation in the semi-tundra conditions of long ago. But long ago that was, and there has been a long and continuous process of change in climate, environment and in the hazel's own evolution ever since. So there must be factors of all kinds that have created a sort of defined zone for a tree that is, generally speaking, a widespread tree. But there are areas outside this zone where there is a certain density of hazel and these are a clue to part of the process. In general they are areas of deciduous woodland, most specifically of oak, such as parts of Eastern Aberdeenshire, and this corresponds with the predominant type of woodland in the greater domains of hazel to the west.

The hazel is rare or absent where the land is dominated by the features of conifer forest and moorland – the pine, the juniper, the birch and the heather. It is most numerous where soil is more rich and complex and less acid, where the ground cover is of grasses and woodland-type leafy herbage, and a mix of deciduous trees. Among trees its principal companion or host is the oak, and wherever there are oak woods the hazel is almost certain to be. It may grow in dense clusters or belts around the oak wood, or sparsely scattered here and there within the wood, or more or less equally mixed with oaks.

The oak woods developed a few thousand years after the early colonisation by hazel, and with the changes they created, or were a part of, the hazel evolved correspondingly. Hazel became a component of a 'new' habitat rather than just ground cover on otherwise near-empty landscapes. However, in adapting itself to the 'new' habitats it did not entirely withdraw from the regions and localities which continued to retain the older features of the landscape. Thus even today, there are sizeable areas beyond the natural regions of the 'newer' trees where hazel is still dominant.

Dense copses and belts of hazel can be seen on the extreme western coasts where oak and other large trees are non-existent or at least very rare, from the west of Mull to the south-west of Sutherland.

In such locations, and in the even more remote habitats of outlying islands where they can be found growing singly or in very small groups, hazels are small and of irregular shape, frequently multi-stemmed. In more sheltered locations they usually have one main trunk and are only multi-stemmed as a result of coppicing. The trunk may be nearly two feet in diameter and the tree may exceed 30 feet in height, although they are commonly leaning so that height above ground is often much less than the actual length of the tree.

A mature trunk is usually twisting and knobbly and pitted, with a rough peeling bark of dark greyish brown. However, it is commonly obscured by a matt of moss. The upper limbs, as well as the trunks of young specimens and the stems of coppiced specimens, are a slightly shiny silvery gold, with a darkening towards the outer limbs. Colour however, is very variable and even on a single specimen the overall appearance of silvery grey or golden brown is seen, on close inspection, to be made up of a mottled patchwork of many subtle shades.

The leaves are more or less round, sometimes slightly oval with a sharp tip. They are toothed and fairly rough, and can be large, particularly on young coppice stems and on the narrow shoots that grow from the base of the trunk of uncoppiced specimens. The winter buds are sometimes reddish brown, sometimes green and sometimes a bit of both. They begin to open in late March, and the leaves, having yellowed slightly, can remain on the tree until late November. Of all non-evergreens hazel are the longest in leaf.

The tree's male catkins are conspicuous throughout the winter and open very early in the year, usually about mid-February. When fully open the drooping catkins are three inches long or more, and usually a yellowish green though sometimes slightly brown. This distinction can be observed between two neighbouring trees. The female flowers appear slightly later, usually not until March and though not very conspicuous are very bright in colour, little tufts of cherry red crowning some of the buds.

From these tiny flowers, when pollinated, grow the fruits of the tree — the well known hazel nuts. Until late summer their shells are green and soft, protected by the enclosing crests of the case or cup. In September they turn brown and outgrow the case and by late October almost all have fallen. They are produced sometimes singly, sometimes in clusters of two, three or more. On good specimens in the best situations — where the soil is good, the light and shelter adequate — many nuts are produced, but of course many are eaten before germination can take place. Some are eaten by birds, such as pigeons and wrens, some by squirrels and some by mice and voles. Squirrels, mice and voles sometimes actually aid the tree's dispersal by forgetting, or ignoring through lack of need, their buried stores. Various small caterpillars also favour the hazel (and in turn many birds), growing and developing as they feed upon the leaves. In certain locations, in certain years, it seems as if winter has arrived many months too soon, for all the foliage is devoured.

Many plants benefit from the presence of hazel, among them primroses and honeysuckle. It is probably honeysuckle's favourite tree – or it may be more correct to say it is particularly suited to the conditions favoured by the hazel.

The hazel has always been very important to the

Highlander and greatly revered. It has an important and ancient role in mythology and custom which is parallelled and contributed to by its great array of uses and benefits, most of which have no traditional taboos restricting them. One certain reason for this lack of taboos associated with a tree that is sacred is its powers of survival, for not only is its coppice growth vigorous but its life can actually be increased by many years, even doubled, when coppiced.

In the traditions of hazel coppicing they are cut about every eight years, when there are many stems suitable for many special uses. From them were made hurdles — pieces of woven fencing for enclosing gardens and for protecting sheep, cows and other livestock with their young. Hazel stems were also used for supporting roofing of thatch and of turf, for making creels and baskets and, sometimes cut low to include the bend towards the root, for making shepherd's crooks and walking sticks. The shinty players of the Isle of Iona used to make their sticks from hazel stems cut on neigbouring Mull. Presumably shinty sticks were made from hazel in many other areas.

The stems of hazel also have had, and in some cases still have, a number of values that lean towards the extraordinary. Perhaps not unconnected with its use as hurdles to protect farm animals and as a crook is the belief that a herding stick of hazel protects cattle from illness. It also had the distinction of being the perfect weapon for killing snakes. It is possible that these functions relate, in a roundabout way, to its almost certain function as a Druid staff of divination and power. And in turn this must correspond to its longstanding importance to dowsers divining for water.

Again relating to the tree's benefits to farm animals are the leaves. It was long believed that as food for cows they would increase milk yield. The nuts, of course, are of direct food value to us and at odd times throughout history they must have been a life-saver. It is on record that King Robert Bruce's garrison at Tarbert, Loch Fyne were under orders to forage far and wide to gather hazel nuts for winter storage. A common custom was to dry and grind them and then mix with flour. They have also been used, because of their oil, for polishing wood.

Hazel nuts, like the stems, also have a significance beyond the immediately understandable. In fact even more so. They epitomise the hazel's principal symbolism in Celtic mythology — that of wisdom. The Gaelic word *chno* or *cno* means the hazel nut, and the Gaelic word *cnocach* means wise. There is an old Gaelic verse that translates:

Thou nut of my heart,
Thou face of my sun,
Thou harp of my music,
Thou crown of my sense.

With various versions the hazel nut's gift of wisdom is portrayed in the ancient Highland tales. The seeker or wanderer comes upon the pool of a spring, about which grow nine hazel trees. Wisdom may come by eating a nut that has fallen into the pool, or by eating salmon from the pool that have been feeding there.

Birch

The birch tree is the most numerous of all our natives. It has exceptional hardiness and virility, representing in many ways the general adaptability and strength in all trees.

Although it has not been depleted so severely as some other forest trees, such as oak and pine, it is not nearly as numerous as it was two centuries ago. The birch has been widespread and prolific for at least nine thousand years. When the great forests-to-be of oak and of pine were still in their youth, slowly developing in the glens and straths of the mountainous regions, the birch was already established in density, even to the extremes of the Outer Isles and the Northern Isles.

Climatic change has caused the birch to withdraw from these extremes. But everywhere its decline has been aided by man — originally in land clearance for agriculture, then in felling along with other forest trees for large-scale metal production, and more recently in clearing for plantations of introduced conifers and, perhaps most significantly, in relatively gradual decline caused by greatly increased sheep farming.

Many birch woods are now no more than threadbare relics of a few old specimens. "Many of them," wrote Fraser Darling earlier this century, "show no regeneration and thus will disappear within a few years because birch is a comparatively short-lived tree."

The common form in the east is the silver birch and in the west the downy or hairy birch.

Yet in some places it is thriving again, being quick to colonise any available ground, spreading quickly on the borders of conifer plantations, by roads and by lochs, and in any areas newly fenced. The birch could hardly be called a threatened tree, though its importance as a coloniser and as a preparer of ground for other plants make its widespread survival very desirable. So many things of nature, plant and animal, favour its presence and fortunately for them it grows well in a wide variety of conditions.

Birches can seed and survive where no other trees will grow, scattered on high acid-soil moors and low poorly drained bogs, and clinging to mountain ridges at an altitude of nearly 2,000 feet, sharing virtually microscopic traces of soil with the rowan. Yet they thrive in the rich deep earth of fertile glens, and in meadows by river and by loch, in ground of lime or clay or sand.

Birch is common in the less exposed parts of Sutherland and Caithness, in the western glens of Aberdeenshire and Angus, and by the freshwater lochs of Perthshire, Argyll and Wester Ross, and especially common on Speyside, by Loch Ness, Loch Garry, Loch Linnhe, Loch Fyne and Loch Awe, and in the lands of Tayside. It is also in surprising abundance on some of the stony, windswept shores on the western fringes, growing in density right to the line of high tide and in dense thickets on virtually every island from Islay to the Uists.

Placenames incorporating the Gaelic name for the tree *beithe* are very numerous, names such as Dunbeath Water in Caithness, Glen an Bheithe, Argyll, Beith in Sutherland, Loch a Bhealaich Bheithe, Inverness-shire and Tall Beith, Perthshire. In old Norse the birch is Bjork, and is similar in the Scots tongue as Birk, as in Birkhall and

Birken Hills.

The ecological contribution made by a forest of birch, whether as a pioneer plant or as a long-term principal plant, has a great influence on the subsequent variety of plants and creatures. As a pioneer it helps to create a habitat for oak or for pine, and where it has remained more or less the principal tree it is the host of a vast array of life forms — bracket fungus, amanita mushrooms and boletus mushrooms, lichens, mosses and ferns, wood sorrel, garlic and cress, hyacinth, primrose and violet, mice, stoats and badgers, woodcocks, robins and redstarts.

Of course the variety of its companions is affected by its geographical and geological situation, depending upon altitude, local climate and soil. The variations can be witnessed in close proximity for in many parts of the Highlands all the diverse habitats of the birch exist within an area of a few square miles. In but half a day's walking one can see the tangled birches, covered in the pale green of lichen, standing in tight groups on the low peat bogs, and the tall, graceful bright-limbed birches of the riverside meadows and fertile slopes. The great wide-trunked old specimens can be seen clinging to, and indeed holding together, the steep, tumbled hillsides. Shiny dwarf birches clothe the high ridges and heaths, and the low dense birch forests crowd the windswept coasts.

It is a fungus growth living in the branches that causes the dense twig clusters sometimes called witch's broom. These clusters look rather like birds' nests, and may be numerous on mature trees.

As already mentioned the birch may grow in solitude or as a pioneer or as a climax plant, yet it is also a companion to other forest trees, growing here and there in forests of oak or pine. Single birches are to be seen in the pine forests of the Eastern and Central Highlands and in the oak forests of the south-west.

But just as these forests have their geographical inclinations there are particular forms of birch that favour particular regions. The geographical separation is not strictly defined but generally speaking the common form in the east is the silver birch and in the west the downy or hairy birch. These forms are recognised as distinct, as is the sub-species called dwarf birch, but the distinctions are slight and the features of reproduction and most laws of growth do not vary.

Presumably each type evolved from one common ancestor. Yet though the birch desired or needed to diversify itself the resulting individual forms retained the original system of reproduction and could thus crossbreed. For some reason individuals remained individual yet alike, creating hybrids yet retaining a distinctly separate form with distinct inclinations. If a young seedling of downy birch were taken from ground in the extreme west and replanted in the east in an area typical of silver birch it may not live a long and healthy life, and vice versa. Nevertheless such exactness of habitat is not common in the Highlands and few locations allow only one exact form of birch. In most of the areas where birch is especially prolific hybrid forms are to be found, and in many areas silver birch, downy birch and in-between hybrids are found close together, and in some areas all are hybrids.

One of the most significant conditions maintaining separation of forms is rainfall, and to an extent the degree of drainage. Downy birch favours the wetter climate of the west and silver birch favours the drier east. Downy birch, though silver must withstand the colder winters of the east, is slightly the hardier and withstands a greater variety of conditions. Among the subtle differences between the two is a difference in pollen structure, enough to be noticed under a microscope yet too slight to prevent crossbreeding. Close inspection of the twigs reveals another. Those of the downy have a surface of fine white 'hairs', hence its name.

The most obvious special feature of silver birch is the pendulous form of drooping or weeping of the long twigs in mature trees. Its bark is indeed more obviously silver, or white, than the bark of downy birch, but the colouring of the latter is very variable. An extra aid to identification is the silver birch's black diamond shapes on the trunk. The twigs of both are a type of maroon and when young both types are more or less this colour all over. But downy birch twigs often remain predominantly maroon into maturity. Both reach a height of about 40 feet, occasionally over 60 feet, but in general silver birch are taller than downy.

The sub-species called dwarf birch is generally considered to be most closely related to downy, and is more likely to cross with downy than with silver. In certain conditions, particularly at a high altitude, it is difficult to distinguish pure dwarf birch from young or stunted individuals of the two greater types. Dwarf birch are specially adapted to conditions of high altitude and/or windy positions, yet such locations do not strictly deny the presence of the greater birches.

Nevertheless many colonies of birch can be seen, some in high mountain folds, some on low coastal ridges and cliffs, that are immediately identifiable as dwarf birch. Such copses are apparent by their uniformity, by the regular form and sameness of the close individuals.

In a habitat suited to dwarf birch individual immigrant silver and downy birch are generally stunted, twisted and of irregular distribution, while the dwarf birches are close and uniform, forming forests in miniature. Here and there throughout the Highlands, separate from the greater birch forests yet in many cases very close, these little forests clothe rocky, windswept ridges, fringe high heaths and fill high mountain corries.

The hardiness and adaptability and sheer proliferation of the birch have ensured that whatever its values to us they are at least readily available. And its values, like its habitats, are many and varied. There are other large hardwoods more valued for special uses, but part of the reason for the comparatively obscure reputation of the birch is in fact its very availability and its prolific seeding. It has never required the preservation and encouragement accorded to other trees.

One of its most significant uses has been as a source of heat, more widely available than other wood if a bit less hot and lasting than some. It has been used not only in the home but as charcoal for fuel in furnaces. The timber has been quite commonly used for indoor woodwork, including furniture, bowls and bobbins, and recently as chipboard, but rarely for outdoor work as it is fairly quick to rot. The birch broom has long been the means of moving dust from floors and leaves from gardens, and of course putting out fires. That the birch broom is a means of putting out a fire is a paradox for the twigs of birch are about the best kindling there is!

A less well known value of the tree is the use of its sap. As usual in a fast growing tree the sap is easily tapped, and among the products of the sap there has been preservative oil, shampoo (known to have been used in Kintail, Wester Ross, in living memory) and even wine (now making a comeback). The same properties of the tree, and its availability, made it suitable for the production of wood-alcohol to be used as an industrial cleanser. And like alder its charcoal was used in gunpowder manufacture, a widspread industry in the Highlands during and after the Napoleonic War.

Occasionally living birches have been used to create fencing. The lower branches are tied or twisted onto those of the neighbouring tree when the trees are semi-mature, but otherwise the fence is very basic. It is created with little effort and requires a minimum of maintenance. Thus though it is not as efficient as a true hedge, it is easy on time and cost — cheaper, longer-lasting and more attractive than a post and wire fence.

The uses of the birch, as with some other species of tree, have not been widespread in time and geography. But every value of this tree, great or minor, has been exploited virtually without detriment to long-term economy or ecology, as the tree is prolific and hardy. There have been periods of over-exploitation, such as the massive smelting for the sake of new industry and war in the latter part of the eighteenth century and the beginning of the nineteenth, but only the last hundred years or so of intense sheep farming has had a real and lasting effect on reducing the density of the Highland birch forest.

Many of the tree's uses are well represented in mythology and folk lore, and many of its general features and habits. More than any other tree it has been a symbol of fertility, and has represented renewal, human and non-human reproduction, and love. Its grace of form has been likened to a beautiful woman, and the poet Coleridge called the birch the lady of the woods. Many old Scots songs of love refer to the birch, such as The Birken Tree and Afton Water. The latter, the words of which were written by Robert Burns, refers to the "sweet scented forest of birch", evoking the romantic setting with reference to the strange scent of the tree when it comes to full leaf in May. Traditionally May is the month of love, as recorded in ancient tales and surviving virtually to the present day in seasonal ritual. In some tales and in some customs its dual symbolism of fertility and romantic love is as one.

In a tale from Dunbartonshire a young princess runs away from her home and meets an elven prince deep in the birch forest. Romantic love and physical desire overwhelm them. Not so very long ago in Scotland youths and maidens, following ancient customs, would pair off and go into the birch forest on the first day of May, and there was a time when adult men and women were free to ignore marriage vows on that particular day. There is an old Welsh poem in which the speaker attempts to persuade a beautiful nun that her vow of chastity can be forgotten in the month of love.

Is it true, the girl that I love,
That you do not desire the birch, the strong growth of
*   summer?*
Be not a nun in spring,
Ascetism is not as good as a bush.
As for the warrant of ring and habit
A green dress would ordain better.
Come to the spreading birch,
To the religion of the trees and the cuckoo.

On the first of May — the Beltaine festival of the Gaels — the age-old rituals and the newer or adapted customs of more recent times were all practised with the intention of harnessing the rampant powers of fertility. And imitation was seen as the means of achieving this. In different ages and different regions the principal rituals have varied from sombre and occasionally bloody acts to innocent customs. But, apart from most modern festivities, a feature common in every case was the dawn fire. In the cold dark of night all hearth fires were put out, to be rekindled only by a brand from the great ritual fire when it is set alight with the rising of May's first sun. The fire was of birch and oak, or just oak, but always kindled with birch twigs. As already mentioned the twigs of the birch are ideal for kindling a fire, but their use in this tradition reflected the supposed beneficial influences of the tree, and it seems probable that the combination of birch and oak in the making of ritual fires symbolised the interaction between the Earth and the Sun.

The life-giving powers of the tree have been invoked in a variety of ways, using all of its parts, and with a number of specific purposes, including the health of livestock. For centuries Highland people believed that if a barren cow was herded with a birch stick it would become fertile, or that a cow in calf similarly herded would produce a healthy offspring. Yet, though the tree was believed to represent or be a medium for the essential forces of continuity and growth, it shared with certain other trees an 'other-worldly' character. Its role as the tree of romantic associations links its earthly functions with its role as a medium for enchantment. Such a link is revealed in tales like that of the meeting between the mortal princess and the immortal prince in the birch forest.

Without the acceptance of only thin, insubstantial borders between separate roles or associations, the diverse properties of the birch, as presumed by our ancestors, appear contradictory. How, for instance, did a tree worshipped for its associations with propagation also become associated with death? It was once a custom to strew a funeral path with birch branches, a tradition observed in Appin, Argyll, within the last hundred years.

But the contradiction is removed when consideration is given to the beliefs behind the customs. To people of the past the imitation of interaction between earth and sun represented by the ritual fire was perfectly in keeping with the representation of the link between this world and the next as observed in funeral rites.

Such observations of traditional practices associated with the birch are drawn from many eras and many regions. It is therefore wrong to imply that across all parts of the Highlands and through thousands of years there existed a uniform, complex and unchanging system of worship and custom involving this, or indeed any other, tree. It is probable that the Appin folk of a hundred years ago who carried their deceased along a path of birch twigs did not indulge in promiscuous behaviour every May the first, and perhaps Bronze Age people did not herd cows with birch sticks even though they surely had beliefs in the magic of the birch.

Of course unavailability in specific regions must have restricted use of birch. Even so, a continuity of attitude did prevail over expanses of time and of space, in particular the romantic and/or reproductive implications of the tree's character. Perhaps the factor linking the romance of the heart with reproductive activity is attraction, for attraction is a part of falling in love and also an important ingredient in the propagation of species, be they human, animal or plant. Thus the birch tree, by its graceful appeal, is suitably acknowledged in custom and mythology as the companion, medium and background for love.

To say that this has been the case because the birch is the most attractive of trees would be a sweeping statement, and indeed mythology has sometimes incorporated other trees into tales of love, notably the hawthorn and the rowan. Yet there are birch features of rare and special appeal, from the subtlest, belonging to the individual specimen, to the greater aspects of the birch forest. There are the tiny glossy catkins of early spring, that open revealing shades of green and yellow and scarlet; the smooth bark, silver, white and maroon; the fine tracery of the crown, upreaching or cascading; the emerald of the diamond-like leaves in early summer and the sunshine yellow of the leaves in autumn; and in winter the copses and high woods of dwarf birch are deep, glossy maroon against the brown of bracken and the grey of stone.

Warriors and Guardians

Rowan

The rowan tree, more so than any other, is at the heart of the Highlander's remaining tree lore. In tales from the past it is one of the most magical of plants, and today there are still many people who will not cut down, or even trim, a rowan. The bad luck such an act is believed to bring is a remnant of belief in the sacredness, or magic, of most white-flowered trees, such as hawthorn and elder. But the rowan has an extra mystique.

It may be argued that all taboos are based upon practical requirements — and of course there is a direct connection — but the reverence shown to the rowan proves that this has not been the sole reason. The taboo against harming rowans outweighs the practical benefits of the tree. Of course to some extent the importance of the taboo has restricted the possible uses. But whereas with other trees taboos are fairly specific and allow other benefits to be fully exploited, the restrictions on using rowans are not balanced by the acceptable uses. Tradition does not allow the use of the tree's timber, bark, leaves or flowers, nor the cutting of these, except for sacred purposes under special conditions.

As far as I can ascertain there has never been a taboo against plucking and using the berries however, and indeed the products of them, notably wine and jelly — rowan jelly is a traditional accompaniment to game — have been of great value in the Highlands.

Tradition does not allow the use of rowan's timber, bark,
leaves or flowers...except for sacred purposes.

There are still many people who would not even trim a rowan that was overhanging a garden, let alone chop one down, yet the timber and the branches have strength and pliancy and could have had, without the taboos, significant value to builders, farmers and craftsmen. The rowan also coppices well.

For some reason, or reasons, the tree has no traditional use of straightforward practical benefit, other than the processing of its berries. It could be said that even this one use was reason enough for the restrictions, considering that the rowan is not a forest tree and is spread only thinly.

Yet there are parts, where rowans are very numerous and where the reverence shown to it is still strong. Besides which, if the taboos were created solely to protect its future it would be incongruous to allow or accept the plucking of the fruits. If the superstitions have anything to do with protection of the rowan's continuity then it was not for straightforward everyday benefits, but for maintaining the beneficial qualities of its spirit.

Uses that recognise the inner qualities have survived almost hand-in-hand with the taboos, and within living memory twigs of rowan have been cut to be above a doorway as protection against misfortune. In the past the cutting, carrying and placing of rowan twigs would have been accompanied by special ritual, and correct timing would have been observed.

As well as threshold protection the twigs have been of importance in farming life. As a stick or switch, for leading cattle, rowan was believed to protect the beasts from hunger. A threshing tool of rowan, called in Gaelic *buaitean*, was used for threshing grain to be used for special occasions. Many of these occasions — times of seasonal and/or astronomical transition — incorporated as a part of the ceremonies the eating of sacred cakes. On some or even most of these occasions the baking of the cakes was done with a fire of rowan wood, although at no other time, and for no other purpose, was rowan wood burnt, unless it were for acts of divination, or perhaps funeral pyres.

This last is quite likely to have once been a use, for not long ago biers of rowan were used in Highland funeral processions. In fact the rowan has a strong customary connection with death, though not usually in a morbid sense.

On the one hand the tree is a protection against death, protecting both humanity and livestock, and indeed other creatures such as a fox in Kintyre. Having reached a cliff when closely pursued by men and dogs, the fox lowered itself to safety by dropping from rowan to rowan. Even the berries have been considered protective, as remembered in a Gaelic saying, which translates, "A black mare kicking among the rocks . . . a handful of red rowan berries to safeguard her."

On the other hand the rowan symbolises death, or rather the after-life, and is a medium between this world and the next. Like some other trees it was thought to be inhabited or presided over by fairies, which with one interpretation are the spirits of the dead, or if otherwise, are at least spirits of immortality. The fairy or guardian spirit of the rowan was believed to counteract the spells of bad witches and to scare off alien fairies. This belief has survived in simplified form, the tree being considered a charm for good luck. Even in recent years rowans have been planted next to new houses.

The origins of all these superstitions are numerous and complex, and probably too much relevant history, myth and tradition have been forgotten for complete answers to be found. In such Celtic mythology that has survived long enough to be recorded we can at least look at the superstitions. They have spread over the centuries, but nowadays the concept of a tree being a good luck charm is the residue of a more esoteric, magical tradition. Like some other trees, yet more so, the rowan was associated with the Celtic Paradise beyond the setting sun, and with *Avalach*, the limbo world between here and Paradise.

There are similarities between the rowan and the apple tree in the age-old symbolic tales and they are indeed closely related botanically. Both grow in places that have been believed to be earthly equivalents of mystical realms (the name *Avalach*, or *Avalon*, has the same root as 'apple'). The sight of one or the other, in constant leaf, flower and fruit, was presumed to greet souls arriving on the Further Shore. In general it seems that in these traditions one is synonymous with the other, interchangeable according to the geographical origins of particular versions. For instance, the apple tree belongs predominantly to tales from south-west England while the rowan belongs to those from the Highlands.

The rowan also features prominently in Irish mythology, much of which, thanks to the clerical writers of Ireland's great scholarly age, was written down. In the already ancient tales and cosmology that these men of the Church recorded, the rowan had affinities with the alphabet, with the calendar, and with all other systems whose creation was based upon observation of the natural world. These systems were supposed to have been inspired by priests or seers that had stepped outside the mortal world, beckoned by a radiant lady bearing a branch with "silver leaves (the underside of rowan leaves are silvery green) and white blossom." What events of the distant past gave the tree this magical status are beyond our memory and understanding and we cannot with any certainty claim that all such tales have no historical basis. Yet there are some observable features of the tree that must have had some bearing on its special status.

The rowan is often called mountain ash because, although not actually related, it has a similar leaf-formation to the ash tree. They will grow at a greater altitude than all other trees — up to 2,000 feet — and this closeness to the realm of the gods must have been one of the reasons for the rowan's sacred status. Another relevant factor may well have been the discovery of rowans growing on other living trees. If you look hard in a Highland oak forest you will almost certainly find a large tree that has a little rowan growing where the trunk forks, or in the crook of a branch. The discovery of a rowan on an oak would have been of special significance, but any combination, such as rowan on ash or rowan on hazel, would have had a special meaning to the finder. The alliance had a relevance similar to that of mistletoe and oak.

The 'parasite' is a plant with the full faculties of growth and regeneration yet does not require soil and is as much a compliment to, as user of, its guardian tree. This feature alone, of being able to grow where soil seems non-existent, on a tree or on a rock face, must be a part of the rowan's special magic. It seems reasonable than an ancestor seeing a rowan in its glory of blossom or berry thriving on bare stone should consider the tree to have affinity with supernatural powers.

A poet or bard would not necessarily have had to be especially philosophical about such a sight, however. He would have found immediate inspiration in such a setting, moved by both the gentle grace of the tree and the strength of its determination to flourish. A specimen growing from the merest crack in a bare cliff of granite may have all of two feet circumference to its pale grey trunk, and if it is surrounded by hazel and birch, as is common in the south west Highlands, its trunk may be three feet in circumference, its growth being enriched by the presence of other trees.

The appeal of the rowan's appearance had, as much as any other feature, relevance to its role in fanciful tales, and its appeal is still recognised. It is commonly planted in gardens, in parks, and by roads, and a mountain scene with a rowan in berry is a favourite image of postcard producers.

Rowans in the wild are of all shapes and sizes. The varying conditions of ground and weather make a great variety of forms, even within a small area. Some are regular with wide trunks and numerous branches and dense foliage. Some are multi-stemmed, short and shrub-like. Some are narrow and twisting and with few branches. Yet in planned conditions the rowan is predictably regular, with smooth trunk, upreaching branches and a fine, rounded crown. The graceful leaves, growing in sets with six or seven pairs and one tip-leaf, will be close and dense on a 'perfect' specimen, and the tree will appear like a green ball on a straight, smooth trunk.

In these conditions the clusters of white blossom will be regularly dispersed over the sphere, and thus the subsequent clusters of scarlet berries. The leaves, which begin as a vivid light green then become dark green with silvery undersides, appear in the second half of April. The flowers open between late May and early June. The berries have turned from green to scarlet by late July. Buds, leaves, flowers and berries are all important sources of sustenance to insects, beasts and birds. Many flies feed on the flowers, and others feed on the berries and lay their eggs in them. Birds like the rowan, some of which go for the berries and others which eat the insects that congregate there. Birds like the Scottish crossbill and the capercaillie, both as Scottish as the rowan, like the young buds and the fruit of the tree. Deer also like the buds after a hard winter, and the young leaves have been gathered by man to feed lean goats.

The process from flowering, through fertilisation, germination, and shooting, is fairly vigorous. The rowan can grow on wide meadows, on damp heaths, vertical cliffs, rocky peaks and windswept moors, and thus in spite of the dangers that it shares with all other trees in this day and age, its future in the Highlands is fairly secure. Everything about it makes it ideal for a Highland situation. After 10,000 years here it is perfectly adapted, not just tolerant of, but dependent upon, prevailing conditions. Thus, while the buds can survive the harshest winter the berries, or rather the seeds within them, must have freezing temperatures before they will germinate. Even within particular regions local rowans are specially adapted to survive. A seed or seedling from the warmer, wetter west would not do well in the colder, drier east, and vice versa.

Reflecting the wide spread of the rowan, and presumably its fame and sanctity, placenames referring to it are more numerous than of other trees. The name 'rowan' is probably from the Norse *reynir,* and in old Gaelic it is *luis,* but its common Gaelic name is *chaoruin.* This word is frequent on the map, with names such as Ben Chaorunn in Inverness-shire, Meall a'chaorun in Wester Ross, Loch a'chaorun in Easter Ross, Cnoc a Chaoruinn on Islay and Loch Chaoruin in Mid-Argyll. One place perhaps using the old word *luis* is Ardlui on Loch Lomond.

The name Lochranza on the island of Arran is said to derive partly from the Norse word for rowan. In that part of Arran there are two totally unique forms of rowan — or rather of the genus *sorbus*, which includes rowan and whitebeam. These, by their leaf formation, appear to be a mid-way stage between rowan and whitebeam. There are other distinct forms of *sorbus* to be found in Lancashire and in mid-Wales.

Rowans are common in or near oak forests, and in or near pine forests, or where such forests have been until recently. They are most numerous in the west, particularly in Argyll where it is the clan badge of the Malcolms and the McLachlans, but there are many in parts of Angus, Aberdeenshire, Moray and Nairn. They are quite common on most of the Inner Hebrides and on the Outer Hebrides. And in the Northern Highlands they are quite numerous on the islands of sheltered lochs. They also grow in the Orkneys and Shetlands.

Untameable tracts of country, the good soil of wooded country (or what has been wooded country), heavy rainfall, a scarcity of the birds that strip the berries in quantity further south such as the starling, cliffs and peaks free of grazers and browsers, and the traces of human superstition — with these facts and features the Highland rowan has, in relation to so many other native plants, a reasonably secure future.

Rowan

Warriors and Guardians

Pine

The Scots pine is the warrior of the tree world. Most specifically it represents or belongs to the Highland warrior, for only here is it truly native. *Pinus Scotica* as it is known botanically was once native further south, in southern Scotland and much of England, but now its only natural habitat is the Highlands of Scotland.

As one of the principal trees of the great spread of woodland across northern Britain known as the Caledonian Forest its distribution was once much greater than now. Yet the common idea that that forest is now no longer is inaccurate. There are in fact a few large areas of natural pine forest still in existence.

Like past Highland warriors boldly surviving here and there among the mountains, awaiting events after long battles fought against invaders, the pine just holds its own. The worst days are behind, the days of mass felling and burning for timber and to feed distant industry, for open country to graze alien sheep, and to deny refuge to bands of Highland outlaws after the Jacobite risings. Now the pine waits for gradual decline or gradual increase — threatened by negligence but just perhaps with a future, thanks to a few conservationists and wise foresters. It is a joy to be able to see the young pines confidently rising above the grass in the open spaces of the newly secured relics of ancient forests, or above the heather of low heathland where pines have long been absent.

The Scots pine is the warrior of the tree world.

It is an asset of the pine that it can survive and flourish on boggy heath as well as on well drained slopes. Over the centuries it has increased this adaptability by evolving two slightly different forms, broadly speaking one form for the east and one for the west. The eastern form is, in general, regular, wide and full-limbed, while the western form is tall, narrow and virtually devoid of branches for much of its height, creating a sort of umbrella effect.

But the Scots pine does have its weaknesses, not least because it is Britain's only true conifer. Its ideal conditions are rather more defined and specialised than required by other forest trees such as oak and birch and only by wide, dense distribution can it maintain that ideal habitat. It is not at all unusual to find a solitary birch in a dense oak forest or an oak in a forest of birch, but such random dispersal is very unusual for the pine. The seeds that drop or are blown from its cones favour ground already enriched by pine needles, and seedlings do not often fare well where they are dominated by too many other plants.

In or near mature pine forest the undergrowth is quite scant in places due partly to the dense needle cover on the ground and partly to the evergreen canopy above restricting light all year round. In this setting seeds and seedlings can thrive, the only natural inhibitor of any significance being hungry deer in winter, a threat it can withstand only by sheer weight of numbers. A wind-blown seed that lands in rich deciduous forest with typical dense undergrowth is not likely to flourish, nor indeed if it lands on open grassland. But it may do well in certain habitats beyond mature pine forest, particularly on birch heath where the dominant plants — birch and heather — are hospitable to pine. This after all is the same environment that encouraged the birth of the great coniferous forests some eight thousand years ago.

Although the pine demands particular conditions in which to thrive individual planted specimens grow well in diverse habitats. Many such habitats, while not the ideal for the tree, sustain its growth by the benefit of the safety they provide, habitats such as gardens, parks and roadsides, although rarely will the planted specimens produce offspring.

This little paradox that the tree is vulnerable yet adaptable has had a bearing on its associated traditions. Being demanding in certain ways is a part of its strength of character, a character also signified by its great height, broad limbs, and by the fact that it is evergreen. Thus it has been planted for its visual impact, chosen as a marker tree for a number of specific purposes throughout history. In parts of England, even in the south, lone pines and rows of pines are still to be seen marking old roads and paths. In England, as well as in Scotland, rings or clusters of pines mark many ancient cairns, mounds and burial grounds. The pines are not likely to be over 300 years old but to some extent at least their planting probably served an ancient tradition.

In this way its role is similar to that of other evergreens, notably the yew, for as an evergreen it was associated with immortality. But in the Highlands at least, it most especially served to mark the burials of warriors, just as in its natural situation it was a 'witness' to many of their battles. Throughout legend and history many of the most significant battles of Scotland were fought within or close to pine forests, from the Pictish defence against the Romans in Perthshire, Angus and Aberdeenshire to the wars against the Plantagenet and Tudor monarchs of England; from the religious/political wars between the Scottish

Dukes to the last and most tragic Highland battle at Culloden.

After Culloden many Jacobite warriors hid in the ancient pine woods of the Central Highlands, already the 'home' of members of disaffected clans such as the McGregors — who, like others of clan Alpin such as the MacNabs and MacKinnons, had the pine as their clan badge.

The time of Culloden in 1746 was a kind of turning point in the fortunes of the pine. Thereafter land-use began to change drastically, not least because concerns that had little to do with most Highland people saw the potential profits to be gained from the enormous supply of timber for industry. And the resulting open country was suitable for new breeds of sheep. From a military point of view (not divorced from the economic gains) the clearing of vast areas of forest helped to deny outlawed Jacobite sympathisers the shelter and hiding that might have aided another rising against the government.

All the larger relics of old pine forest are now protected and managed as reserves, mainly by Scottish Natural Heritage and Forest Enterprise, but some by private landowners. Among the largest reserves are those at Rothiemurchus, Braemar and other locations around the Cairngorms, Rannoch Moor in Perthshire, Loch Tulla and Doire Darrach in Argyll, Glen Affric in Inverness-shire, and Loch Maree in Wester Ross. The pine is actually most prolific in the eastern Highlands and dense, ancient forests such as at Loch Maree are exceptional in the predominantly broadleaf domains of the west.

However, placenames using the Gaelic word for pine which is *giubhas* are mostly in the west, where the language remained the first for longer — among them Cnoc a Guibhais and Allt a Ghiubhas in Wester Ross, Leac a Ghiubais on Mull, and Glac a Ghiubas, Ardgower. This very fact that the principal domains are in the east away from the strongholds of Gaelic culture has meant that the pine, overall a tree of great importance in the Highlands, has a surprising lack of ancient tradition attached to it. Another factor that has contributed to the general lack of recorded information pertaining to the lore of the pine is the isolation of its domains, even in the past, as relating to the British Isles as a whole.

For most trees occasional references to surviving fragments of custom in the records of the last century or so can be related to the records of England, Wales and Ireland. In this way a fairly comprehensive explanation can be created of a tree's long-term relevance to rural society in the Highlands. The pine, apart from such links as the planting of rows and circles outside its native regions, does not fit into the wider field of Celtic tree lore. In other words, there are few sources from which we can take references to the pine in order to build up a pattern of features that would relate customs to uses, taboos to mythology and history, and so on.

There are however, isolated references that indicate a place of importance in overall tree cosmology, some significant mentions of ancient origin. For instance, the Gaelic alphabet, the letters of which are the first letters of trees and other plants, includes the pine, but not as G (for *guibhas*) but as P for *peith*, an alternative Gaelic word for the tree. There are also legends from Argyll and from the Inner Hebrides (such as Rhum and Eigg) that include the pine, incorporating it into tales of love, war and death. But mention is scant and can appear contradictory. The lack of recent custom and widespread superstition makes the pine's character difficult to explain, compared to other trees widespread in the Highland past.

There are one or two other points which may have contributed to the tree's relatively lowly place in tree lore, or at least in surviving records and memories of tree lore. For a tree of such size and of such natural density it has not had a great many important uses, especially in recent centuries. So much of our recorded tree lore stems from its survival into the nineteenth century but by then the pine was not especially important to the everyday lives of ordinary people. This was partly due to its great decline but also to the growing use of alternative products. Such traditions as planting pines as markers to graves were already virtually a thing of the past and there never were any superstitions of a more domestic nature, as was the case with many other trees — the kind of customs like wearing certain leaves or adorning the house with certain blossoms.

Not only were the uses of pine generally of a more industrial, less everyday, nature, there was no great tradition of pine forest management because the pine does not coppice. Without the sort of ritual customs associated with coppice woodland and because the pine has no direct food value to us or our domestic animals, the tree has had no great part in long-lasting folklore. These points are, however, only relative and the pine does have some special uses and an important role in ancient mythology.

One of its features of greatest value is its resin. This was once tapped or otherwise extracted for a number of specific products, among them a healing ointment, varnish, paint and tar. The tar was of special value to the builders of boats and ships, for sealing the planks and waterproofing the hull. Because of the resinous quality of the tree's timber, and because it is pliant and strong, and because the trunk is commonly tall and straight, the actual planking of boats was often of pine. At the mouth of the River Spey there were busy shipyards during the Stuart era and pine logs were floated down river from the great forests inland.

There was once a superstition among boatbuilders that the tree should not be felled during the wane of the moon. We can guess it was believed that the sap was 'tidal' under the influence of the moon and that the resinous quality of the wood was less during the moon's waning. This is a belief perhaps not without rational basis for botanists now know that fluctuations in sap-flow are complex. The tar was also once commonly used for oil-lamps and reed-lights and, even in areas where the pine had already long since disappeared through natural change, pieces of bog-pine were used for lighting. Usually these would be found during peat-cutting and be broken from ancient logs and stumps preserved by their own resin and by the peat-bogs that replaced the forests.

The pine may not be of direct food value to us but is of great importance to many wild animals, especially some that are exclusive to the Scottish Highlands and others that are relatively common here. There are the deer, the red and the roe, whose traditional environment, especially of the red deer, is pine forest. The new shoots of young trees provide nutrition in winter. With the great decline in such forests at the hands of man the red deer has adapted itself to living most of its life in open country but it is quite a lot smaller than it used to be – such is our awesome power over nature. Then there are the pine marten and the red squirrel, both extremely rare outside of the Highlands, particularly the former. And there are the birds, the exclusively Scottish capercaillie, the crested tit and the Scottish crossbill and the birds of prey, especially the sparrowhawk and osprey. Some of these creatures eat the seeds of the pine cones, some eat the wood-wasps and wood-ants of the pine forest. Others eat the mice and voles that eat the seeds and the insects, while in the case of the rare fish-eating osprey it is the tree as a nesting place that is favoured. Many of the pine forest creatures, for instance deer and crossbill, have adapted well to the environment of alien conifer plantations but not only are these relatively barren habitats, they are temporary and the sudden mass fellings prevent a secure, longterm population.

For most of these creatures and others, there is really no ideal alternative to established, regenerating forests of Scots pine. Such an environment is rich and diverse. There are pines of every size from tiny seedlings to old specimens of 80 feet and more and there are birch trees and junipers and heathers and ferns.

The Scots pine is slow growing for a conifer and its sole form of propagation, by seeding, is slow. It takes two seasons of development before the little cone-like maroon female flowers receive the pollen (insect transferred) from the clusters of short catkin-like yellow male flowers. Then it takes two seasons for the little green cones to become large and brown and woody, ready to release their seeds. During this time parasites and strong winds may greatly reduce seed-production.

This, added to other factors mentioned, is a part of the tree's weakness. Its weaknesses and special requirements are offset to some extent by its strengths and its adaptability but only as a protected tree does it maintain its present spread. Protection in the form of special reserves is very important but is artificial and not really the ideal way to secure a long-term survival. It does not befit the tree's dignity and also denies its existence as a free-ranging tree within the Highlands as a whole. Reserves halt its decline but proper recognition of its uses as well as its requirements could be of enormous benefit to the pine as a thriving species, secure as a thing of the wild and a great boon to man.

Ash

The pale grey ash tree is one of the very largest of trees in the Highlands. There are some particularly large individuals that are larger than any oak or elm or pine — enormous specimens dominant by height and by girth. The form of ash seen here is the European ash, fairly common in many countries, though especially so in regions of high rainfall, and particularly in hilly country of limestone.

Nevertheless the ash is not dependent on lime-rich soil and it survives well on a variety of soils in the Highlands, as elsewhere. It is remarkable that ash trees can reach maximum height and width as easily on stony northern slopes as on rich, gentle agricultural lands to the south. Their need for moisture is unusually great for a large tree (which, relatively speaking, require less than many of the smaller trees). In this way it is more like alder or willow than oak or elm, yet alders and the larger types of willow will not survive high on stony hills.

As the young ash reaches upward and outward its roots spread and tunnel with equal vigour, searching out the underground water that will ensure survival in periods of drought. The tree's great root system and great thirst do not unduly threaten nearby plants, for the roots go deep and do not spread far outward, forcing their way through cracks in the ground-rock rather than 'ploughing' the top soil.

It was once commonly believed that the depth of the ash's roots is equal to its above-ground height. This is of course a generalisation but is not totally inaccurate, and this feature of the tree had a bearing on the tree's special role in Norse mythology.

The ash was *Yggdrasil* — The World Tree — holding in its great roots the whole world and in its upper branches Asgard and the mansions of the gods. The Norse influence has been very great in many parts of the Highlands and Islands and the Norse word for ash *ask*, is not uncommon here, as in the name Port Askaig, Islay. *Ask* is clearly related to the tree's English name, and quite possibly both share origins with the Gaelic name *uinsinn* (usually pronounced 'ooshin'). The word *uinsinn* is fairly common in placenames, particularly so in Argyll, for instance Lan-an-uinsinn, Aird uinsinn and Allt uinsinn.

Ash trees are numerous in much of Argyll, notably

around Loch Fyne and Loch Awe, and in some places it is on the increase. It is also fairly common in Inverness-shire, Dunbartonshire, Perthshire and parts of the north-east. It is thinly scattered in Easter Ross, Wester Ross and on most of the Inner Hebrides, and is rare or absent only in the Central Highlands, the extreme north west, the Outer Hebrides, Orkney and Shetland. It has been quite widely planted (though mostly where it is naturally present) and is common in field boundaries in the rich agricultural regions of the Eastern Highlands, and in almost all parts it has been planted to mark estate boundaries, drives and gateways. Its great height (70 — 100 feet), its hardiness, its speed of growth (considerable for a large hardwood), and its long life (200 years or more) are factors relevant to these uses of the living tree. But they were also compliments to the particular symbolism of the tree in Norse mythology — as a kind of link between Earth and Heaven.

Whether planted as a symbol or for purely practical reasons the fine appearance of the ash is hardly irrelevant. Its pale colouring — a pale grey that is more or less uniform over the whole tree — makes it stand out in winter, and its general shape, with great branches that dip downward then 'curl' upward at the tips, is very distinc-tive. Its pattern of growth is of course variable — it may be low and wide, with a short thick trunk and rounded crown, or it may be tall and lanky with a forked trunk — but, more so than most of the larger hardwoods, it tends to be fairly straight and upright, even where conditions are apparently not ideal. The regularity of form is seen in young saplings, middle-sized trees and very old speci-mens alike.

The notable distinctions in form between young and

old are the outward and upward reach of the branches and smooth trunk of the former and the downward (apart from the upper limbs) and upward reach and fissured trunk of the latter. New leaves on young trees, and sometimes on younger branches of mature trees, are usually a distinctly purple colour becoming bright green.

The leaves grow from a seasonal stalk in three to six pairs (occasionally more) with a single leaf at the stalk's tip. They are late to appear, sometimes not till mid-May, but they often remain on the tree, still bright green, till very late in the year, even well into November, and the yellow/green stalks usually stay on the tree for a while longer. About the time the buds begin to open the little flowers suddenly bloom. The blossoming is not noticeable from a distance but seen close up the flowers are bright and beautiful. In early summer the smooth grey twigs are tinged with many colours — the purple and green of the new leaves, the dusky black/brown of the opening buds, and the black and maroon of the flower tufts.

Male and female organs are together in the flower head (pollination is by wind), but just occasionally one finds an ash that is purely male or purely female. In late summer the clusters of ash keys appear, pale green on hanging stems. The keys are twisted seed-cases with a single seed, designed to be carried easily by the wind. In some years they are plentiful and in some they are few, but the germination rate is high. Quite often clusters of mature brown keys remain on the tree through most of the winter, although after a while these become lifeless, unable to germinate when they eventually fall. The numerous keys formed in a good year, and remaining on the tree through a hard winter, are greatly appreciated by certain small birds, such as the bullfinch, eating the seeds to combat cold and hunger. In fact at all stages of the tree's annual cycle it provides sustenance for the life around it. Spiders and beetles thrive in its leaf-litter, deer eat the buds and the bark of fallen branches, ferns grow in the fork of the trunk and on low branches, and hazels, garlic and primroses grow around it.

The vigour with which it supports itself and its companions was once widely recognised, respected and exploited. Perhaps partly because of its sudden bursting into life in May, partly for its tall strong form and its long life, it was once considered to have a benign influence on the newborn. People used to give sap of the ash tree to newborn babies, and to put green ash twigs on the birth-chamber fire. These customs, and others similar, were common in the Highlands until not so very long ago, and though they may have been practised in blind superstition they may well have had a sound medicinal basis. If such a vast array of creatures, from beetles to deer, so value its sustenance it is reasonable to suppose that the part of the tree most palatable to humans, the sap, should be beneficial to our health. Yet whatever the extent of biological knowledge involved in these old customs the rite itself had its own significance, for the act was done in honour of the tree and the deity or deities that gave it its strength, and was as a prayer made for the newborn child. Long, long ago there were probably several ritual acts practised in honour of the ash, for its benefits and uses were numerous and diverse, unsurpassed in its values by any other tree.

Products of its foliage are dye and animal fodder, its keys can be eaten (pickled), and its sap drunk. Its wood can be made into handles of weapons and tools, sports implements, oars, wheels and ploughs. Our ancestors valued ash for making spear shafts and for felloes or rims of chariot wheels. Pliancy, strength, lasting qualities — these make it ideal for such items of wood, but it is also its habits of growth that create its array of values. It coppices vigorously, and yet tidily, creating a growth of well-spaced more or less uniform limbs. When use of ash in this way was common here, there were a number of ways of harvesting to gain maximum and lasting benefit. A tree of full size could produce a great many straight planks and then the resulting coppice growth could be left for five, ten or twenty years, depending on the requirements of products to be made. For instance five years or less for a pea or bean stick, ten years for a spear shaft, twenty years for a ship's oar. But to add to all these uses, even in a sense to equal them all put together, the wood is the best firewood there is. It burns hot, and lasts, and green wood is almost as good as seasoned wood.

Like all trees it does not have the security in the Highlands that it once had. Nevertheless its position is strong and while it diminishes in one area it increases in another. Its adaptability to varied habitats, including many places where man's activities are actually encouraging its increase, the abundance of its flowering, fruiting and germinating, its strength and resilience — with these qualities the ash is continuing to thrive.

Ash

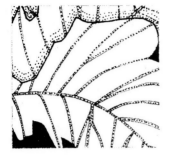

Oak

There are two forms of oak native to the British Isles, the sessile and the pedunculate. They are distinct yet very close. They are more or less geographically separate yet readily cross with one another. The sessile or durmast oak is the usual type of the north and west, and the pedunculate or English oak is the usual of the south and east.

For reasons that will be seen, it is debatable how much of Scotland is within the natural domain of the English oak. It is likely that it is native to most of the south and east and to the southern and eastern fringes of the Highlands.

However, the sessile or durmast is the common form of oak in the Highlands. In general the sessile is slightly the taller and narrower and slightly more resilient than the pedunculate, evolved as it is for slightly harder conditions. But the particular features which most significantly distinguish it from the pedunculate are its acorn cups which have a much shorter stem, and its leaves which grow from an annual shoot rather than directly from the twig.

The leaves and acorns are well known features of the oak and barely require description, yet they are surprisingly varied in size, shape and colour. The lobed leaves which cannot be confused with those of other trees can vary greatly from tree to tree and even from one part of a tree to another. Mature oaks commonly have clusters of thin, short twigs growing from the trunk and the leaves

A coppiced oak, cut every few years, can go on producing timber for centuries.

on them are usually very small and tinged with a deep red colour, similar to the tree's young leaves in general but remaining so throughout the season. This colouring of leaves, on trunk or elsewhere, is locally variable. Thus one tree is bright green in early summer while its neighbour is orange or red. Acorns are not so obviously varied in colour but do vary considerably in full grown size. In general the pedunculate, English, oak produces larger acorns and in greater quantity.

The oak is late to come into leaf, often not until mid-May. There is a second budding in late July or early August, known traditionally as the Lammas budding, Lammas being the Celtic festival of the first day of August. This second growth is most noticeable on the sessile, as it combines an increased growth of the annually produced stems. The acorns reach maturity as early as late August or as late as early October, depending of course, on the season's weather.

Yet the relevant influences are subtle and complex. Certain trees, particularly those in sheltered places, but even those on rocky slopes of poor soil, consistently produce a good crop of acorns. The male flowers on such a tree are prominent in June — dense clusters of long golden catkins, well distributed over the tree. The little red female flowers are only noticeable at close inspection but may be equally numerous. The pollen is carried from male to female by wind.

A forest of oak, or indeed an individual oak, is host to an unsurpassed array of plants and creatures. Among its companion plants are, largest in size, hazel trees and, smallest, a great many forms of lichen. In fact lichens (there are several hundred types) favour oaks above any other tree. The bark of mature oak is often completely obscured by lichen. It is as much the texture of the bark and its water-retaining qualities that the lichens favour as the tree's particular nutritional benefits. Thus lichen growth does not harm the host tree and as a part of the ecology of a whole forest it is actually of benefit to the trees. Lichen, alive or dead, provides nutrition for many of the inhabitants of the forest, from deer to beetles, from lowly plants such as fungi and mosses to the trees themselves.

As a link between all the life-forms, plant and animal, great and small, there are all the insects and spiders that pervade this environment. They are incredibly numerous and varied, sustained by all parts of the oak — bark, wood, buds, leaves, flowers and acorns. For instance, there are the gall wasps that rely upon the twigs, drawing upon the matter of the tree fibre and sap to make the galls that sustain and protect their larvae. One type of gall wasp is the maker of the familiar oak apple.

Many other flying insects feed upon the twigs and leaves and flowers of the tree, some of which, like the gall wasp, also lay their eggs on the oak. Its popularity with insects does not go unnoticed by spiders and oaks are often covered with webs. Many kinds of butterfly also feed upon the aphids and larvae of the oak woods. Most of the insects and spiders and the like contribute to the food supply of birds and small mammals. Oak woods are the favourite habitat of bats, and jays and woodcocks nest there. Then there are mice and badgers, feeding on the acorns as well as the insects. And of course squirrels. Centuries ago wild boar lived among the oaks, eating the acorns and, until quite recently, domestic pigs were let loose among them.

Man has had multiple benefits from the oak and it

would probably be right to say that no other tree has more greatly improved our standard of living. Even the little oak-apples made by the gall wasps have had their value, for ink was extracted from them. The chief component of the ink is tannine, and the special quality and quantity of oak tannine has had a great many special uses. Extracted from the bark, it was the principal source of tannine for the leather-tanning industries. Large quantities of oak bark were sent from the West Highlands to Glasgow for this purpose. Bark and leaves were also valued for cloth-dying, and in early chemical industries.

The leaf mould of the oak is very rich and makes an excellent garden or farm compost, especially for fruit growing. Twigs of oak were once commonly used for brushing teeth — the tannine in them helps to strengthen gums. Then there are all the important uses of its timber: as fuel for the home; as fuel for iron-smelting (usually converted to charcoal) in the furnaces of Bonawe and Furnace in Argyll; for the making of barrels, wheels, doors, tables and roof-beams; and for building ships of war and of trade. Shipbuilding might be said to be the most important and valued use of oak timber. Not only is the wood very hard and long-lasting but the natural shape of the tree provides the forks, crooks and knees to fashion particular boat parts.

Proper management of an oak wood, as is known to have been practised in many parts of the south-west Highlands until this century, provides a potentially in-definite supply of products to serve all the uses and industries mentioned. Such a wood would be a mixture of mature standards, coppices and saplings. A coppiced oak, cut every few years, can go on producing timber for furnaces and for boats for hundreds of years.

In the building of ships, and smaller boats, there are parallels with the ancient character of the oak in mythology and legend. A few centuries ago the Lords of the Isles, rulers of all the Hebrides and a large part of the western mainland, could at any one time muster a fleet of warships numbering several hundred. The main timber for these ships was oak, a commodity in great abundance within the Lords' domains, particularly the western mainland of Argyll, so close to the Islay capital. And many of the boats used by the travelling monks of Ireland and Scotland between ten and fifteen hundred years ago were made of oak. It is said that Saint Brendan, probably the most widely travelled of Celtic saints, received a divine message when he returned from a short-lived sea-exploration to the west, telling him he should replace his skin-covered boat for one of solid oak.

Be that as it may, the very ancient importance of oak was certainly observed and valued by the incoming Christian faith. Columba himself, the greatest of the monks of the Celtic Church in Scotland, cared greatly for oak. He retained a great love for the oak wood of Derry in Ireland (Derry is from the Celtic for 'oak') where he had preached before coming to Iona. On Iona he built a chapel of oak, cut from the great oak woods of neighbouring Mull. And long since, Highland people would bake cakes with only oak as fuel on Thursdays, which is Columba's day.

Of course it did not need tree-worship to see and exploit the qualities of oak, be it for boats, for buildings or for baking. But the characteristics of the tree as a thing of use have traditionally been inextricably linked with those of its symbolic roles. The oak's traditional significance is wide and well documented, yet in spite of this and in part because of it, the tree's symbolic importance is not clear-cut and absolutely defined. Customs of the early Christian period, and those which survived into very recent times, had their beginnings in the religion of the Celtic druids and probably, in part at least, in the religion of the pre-Celtic inhabitants. According to our own mythology and to Roman observers the Druids used the oak for many purposes and used many parts of the tree — leaves for a crown, a branch for a staff, wood for sacred fires and for making sacred effigies. And they worshipped among oaks.

The use of oak for sacred fires had its origins in the distant past but was still observed here in the last century, perhaps into this century. A log of oak burning was the focal point of the festivities and ceremonies of most of the year's special times, such as the Beltaine festival of May the first, the Midsummer Solstice and the Winter Solstice.

A number of factors gave oak this role to play, both practical and symbolic, one of which was the attraction it has to lightning and its readiness, relatively speaking, to go on fire unaided by man. It was once believed, or at least romantically supposed, that mistletoe grew from a seed put there by lightning, where the bolt of the Thunder God touches the oak.

Mistletoe is certainly not confined to oak trees but its discovery there has been especially important, complementing the symbolism of the oak on which it grows in a number of ways. Its golden flowers have been likened to the sun and in this feature, as in the oak's attraction of lightning and its use as fuel for special fires, lies the link between its magical and religious roles and that of its status as the symbol of kingship.

This character of the oak has been important to people in many parts of the world, from Greece to Japan, and from Brittany to the Hebrides. The Lords of the Isles, Kings in their own domains, sailed the seas in ships of oak. King Arthur was buried in a hollowed oak log, oak leaves are the badge of the royal clan Stewart and Ossian, the bard famed throughout Ireland and the Scottish Highlands, said of the late King of Strumon,

The green-spreading oak is his bower,
Fair growing and lovely and lasting . . .

The life of the oak represents in so many ways the looked-for qualities of a ruler. It has size and strength and long life. It reaches fullest leaf about mid-summer when the sun is at its strongest. And sometimes there are oaks that still have leaves not totally browned about midwinter when traditionally the old King dies and the next is born. There is apparently a kind of triangle here of king — oak — sun, a relationship made of superstition and complicated symbolism yet also of plain observation and practical need.

There is need as in keeping warm, as in the aptly-named need-fires made in summer by Highland people over thousands of years. At the seasonal ceremony the sacred oak log was burnt, although not always until it was totally consumed. An old oak log found in a central part of North Uist is supposed to be the sign of a place once used for such festivities and the place is named after the oak — Sail Dharaich.

Dharaich or *darroch*, is a form of the general Celtic name for the oak like *der* is in Welsh and *durr* or *derry* in Irish Gaelic. Among other places in the Highlands named after the oak are Doire Darach on Mull, Carraig-nan-darroch on Colonsay, Ardarroch in Wester Ross, Craigendarroch in Aberdeenshire and Clashindarroch in Banffshire.

The general spread of the oak is from south west Sutherland to south west Argyll and the island of Arran, through Western Perthshire and Western Aberdeenshire. Among the places where there are large areas of oak are Moidart, Loch Eil, Sunart, — these being in Lochaber where the oak leaves are the badge of clan Cameron — Mid-Argyll, Loch Lomond, Loch Katrine, Loch Tay and Braemar. And there are isolated but significant forests of oak in the north-east, such as on the Dornoch Firth.

In some of these areas there are oakwoods protected as reserves, some of which are as large as any equivalent forest anywhere, and there are many isolated patches and remnants of great age (five or six thousand years). Even on extremely exposed peninsulas in the west there are stretches of dwarf oak forest, the trees curled and stunted by the winds but constantly thriving. But they are only thriving well where they are more or less inaccessible to man and his animals on those wild promontories and within nature reserves.

The oak has a degree of security in the Highlands as a whole but there are large areas of the country where it was once common but is now rare or gone altogether. In the light of what it has meant to us over centuries upon centuries, in practical use and in imagery, a wish for its continuing presence and partial increase here and there seems justified.

Oak

Warriors and Guardians

Afterword

As to the spread of native tree cover in the Highlands and Islands of Scotland, compared to what has been and what should ideally be, this book paints a rather gloomy picture. Areas of ancient forest and the continuity of individual species are indeed under threat.

The removal of the threat and the fulfilment of the ideals of beauty and fertility in harmony with a sustainable economy is a current concern of many people. Local authorities, conservation bodies, large companies, landowners, community groups — all of these hold the future of native tree cover in their hands. Even just a few years ago the attitudes and actions of many of the relevant organisations and individuals did not indicate grounds for optimism. But it is true to say that great changes have been afoot more recently.

The woodman of the past — the *coillear* — would not have comprehended the vast gulf that has opened between the requirements of land productivity and the less tangible ideals of ecology and landscape quality. "You can't eat scenery!" has been the cry of the people on the land mustering against the threat of conservation measures. Yet in the past the scenery was more beautiful and more verdant than now and the land was more productive.

Such a cry holds only a shallow truth, but it has been in part provoked by a conservation approach that was largely focused on the preservation of the Highlands and Islands as a genetic pool for scientific study. The presence of people was at best unimportant, at worst a nuisance.

The genetic pool is very important. It is important in world terms — the geology, landscape, creatures and plants of the Scottish Highlands and Islands are of huge significance in the global designation of environmentally important eco-systems. In world terms such intensive and extensive eco-systems are vital to the continuity of life. It is vitally important too, to use the scientific expertise that is available. We cannot pretend that current systems of land-use are age-old and proven.

Nor can we safely believe though, that our world-renowned landscape is totally safe in the hands of those that govern, manage and work with it. Its continuity — even though it is integrated with some of the oldest rock in the world — is fragile and prone to change. But change and development need not be halted to allow for the continuity of this heritage. It is in our history that we see this proven. Successive waves of invasion or immigration, or internal cultural and economic change, have been accompanied, in general, by an in-built respect for nature. Certainly periods of imperial expansion and its effects on the environment have been dramatic. But subtler influences are at work too.

Environmentally speaking, imperialist expansion in the Scottish Highlands and Islands has not been very significant. Because of geographical and topographical conditions, and because of determined resistance, there has been a significant continuity of tradition. Lifestyles, beliefs and the human relationship to the natural world have had a beneficial effect on this environment. In spite of two or three centuries of largely negative change, their influence can still be witnessed. Each crisis that has afflicted the region in the modern era — defeat, clearance, famine, exploitation, emigration, religious conflict, abuse of the clan system — has eroded ancient values and attitudes and has hardened the hearts and minds of the people. But there remains an attachment to the land that is rare in the developed world.

In the 'undeveloped' world, the polarisation between the people on the land and the powers-that-be is more defined and obvious and in some ways creates a much simpler conflict. In such places as north-west America and Canada, in South America and in the Himalayan foothills, people have been organising against and defying the short-sighted exploitation of the natural forests by big business or government. In these kinds of locations it has been clear that the survival of local populations and their cultures and the survival of native forests are inextricably linked. But in the modern Highlands of Scotland, an eventful history has created a complex situation requiring effort, negotiation and compromise.

For here, as in the hills of Asia and elsewhere, there has been a long tradition of inseparable mutual sharing between people and trees. The benefits of such a sharing relationship — environmental, economic and social — are becoming widely recognised. Established national organisations such as the Forestry Commission are constantly reviewing their policies and operations. A whole raft of national and local bodies, such as the Woodland Trust, Trees for Life, Scottish Natural Heritage, Scottish Native Woods, Scottish Conservation Projects and the Local Enterprise Companies are making positive contributions.

In addition some regional and district councils are involved in the preservation and enhancement of woodland. And some of the private commercial forestry companies are increasingly allowing for wider benefits and operating in partnership with other organisations.

There have been a number of interesting and hopeful new initiatives launched in recent years. The concept of Crofter Forestry is now a reality and will bring economic and environmental benefits to some of the most outlying areas. Community Woods is a concept now endorsed by a number of bodies. It can mean a small woodland on the edge of a settlement, a brand new wood or a large area of commercial plantation adopted by a community. Caledonian Forest Reserves are being established in many areas, the aim being the protection of ancient natural woodland such as the pine woods of the Central Highlands and the oak woods of the west.

Although in some respects the introduced conifers have been the enemy of native trees, some of the new forest initiatives allow for the continuity of both. The lines between commercial plantation and natural woodland are becoming blurred and this, on the whole, is a good thing. To what extent and on what time-scale our native trees will overtake the introduced trees, remains to be seen. But the important factor is that the different interests are no longer in such a state of conflict.

One initiative that is playing a key role in finding common ground between different interests is Reforesting Scotland. Their wide approach seeks to look at all aspects of tree cover — ecological, commercial, amenity and practical. This way embraces all interests and recognises the rights and input of conservationists (professional and voluntary), forest contractors, forest officers and workers, landowners, crofters, ramblers, tourists, agencies and communities.

The existence and continuity of trees was, to some extent, taken for granted in the past and there seemed little need for drastic measures to ensure that continuity. People did take measures to make certain their local woodlands were regenerating and staying healthy. But there was no need for a sense of urgency. The dwindling of woodland in recent decades and centuries — accompanied by depletion of fertility of the land and changes in our requirements of the land — has created a sense of urgency.

The need to take special action to reverse the situation has initiated an array of policies, schemes, management plans, surveys, practical actions, grants and ideas. All over the country there are regeneration schemes underway and there are now a great many nurseries producing predominantly native trees. The idealism, the will and the energy exists.

Getting it right when there are so many factors, so many concerns and so many organisations is no easy task. What might help to make things better for the future is an acceptance that our predecessors, for all their superstitions, had a practical and meaningful understanding of the relationship between people and trees.

Further reading

A Field Guide to the Trees of Britain and Northern Europe
Alan Mitchell (Collins)

Carmina Gadelica
Alexander Carmichael (Floris Books)

Plants with a Purpose
Richard Mabey (Collins)

The Silver Bough
F Marian McNeill (McLellan)

Natural History in the Highlands and Islands
Fraser Darling (Collins)

Oxford Book of Trees
(Oxford University Press)

Celtic Heritage
A & E Rees (Thames & Hudson)

Index

This is an index of tree species, places and terms used in this book. Words from the Gaelic, Scots and Norse languages have been italicised.